The First Nations of British Columbia

The First Nations of British Columbia
An Anthropological Overview

THIRD EDITION

Robert J. Muckle

UBCPress · Vancouver · Toronto

22 21 20 19 18 17   5 4 3 2

Printed in Canada on paper that is processed chlorine- and acid-free.

ISBN-978-0-7748-2873-4 (pbk.)
ISBN-978-0-7748-2874-1 (pdf)
ISBN-978-0-7748-2875-8 (epub)

Cataloguing-in-publication data for this book is available from Library and Archives Canada.

Canadä

UBC Press gratefully acknowledges the financial support for our publishing program of the Government of Canada (through the Canada Book Fund), the Canada Council for the Arts, and the British Columbia Arts Council.

UBC Press
The University of British Columbia
2029 West Mall
Vancouver, BC V6T 1Z2
www.ubcpress.ca

Contents

Part 6: First Nations and Anthropology in the Twenty-First Century

Appendices

Maps and Illustrations

Acknowledgments

First and foremost, I am appreciative of the many First Nations peoples in the province that have accommodated my passion for anthropology and education over the past few decades. I was fortunate in my formative years as a professional anthropologist to have enormous support from several First Nations, especially among the Secwepemc. I am particularly grateful to former chiefs Edna Louis and Nathan Matthew (Simpcw), Ron Ignace (Skeetchestn), and Gerald Etienne (Bonaparte), whose support of my initial work gave me credibility that led to many other projects for First Nations in British Columbia.

I have been fortunate in my career to have had dozens of opportunities to be part of anthropology programming for First Nations students, both on- and off-reserve, and in First Nations institutions as well as public colleges and universities. I place a high value on the institutional encouragement and the support from the First Nations students I have taught. I have also learned much from these students, who often offer insight into their lives and cultures. I am especially grateful in this regard to Syexwaliya/Ann Whonnock (Squamish Nation), Jamie Thomas (Snuneymuxw), and Yumks/Rudy Reimer (Squamish Nation).

I have also benefited from the opportunity to learn from many First Nation community members. Paramount in this regard are Rhiannon Bennett (Musqueam) and Sonny Assu (We Wai Kai). Rhiannon schooled me, in a very respectful way, about the complicity of archaeologists and anthropologists in inadvertently undermining First Nations, through their actions, inactions, and use of language. Besides my appreciation of his art for its aesthetic, meaningful, and thought-provoking qualities, Sonny has significantly influenced my thoughts on colonialism and the arbiters of authenticity. I also give thanks to both Rhiannon and Sonny for speaking to my students and providing some measure of support for my own work.

For their constructive feedback on previous editions of this book, I would like to thank the reviewers of the manuscripts for the first and second editions, including Rene Gadacz, Rick Blacklaws, Patricia Shaw, and several anonymous reviewers. I also appreciate the insightful comments and suggestions from several anonymous reviewers of the proposal for this edition of the book.

As a non-First Nations person writing about First Nations, I open the door to criticism from First Nations. I am thankful that the vast majority of comments I have received on the two previous editions from First Nations people, including students, community members, and colleagues, have been overwhelmingly positive. Without that endorsement, this edition of the book would not have been written.

Many anthropologists have aided my professional development and relationships with First Nations, which have ultimately led to this book. Archaeologist Dr. Roy Carlson (Simon Fraser University) was the person who first opened the door for me to work with First Nations, and I am appreciative for that initial opportunity. Much of my early professional work was with anthropologist Dr. Marianne Ignace (Simon Fraser University), who really introduced me to the culture of anthropologists working among First Nations. My colleague at Capilano University, Dr. Gillian Crowther, has similarly been a valuable resource based on her own field work working with First Nations and teaching about them in classrooms. I also appreciate the support of my other departmental colleagues at Capilano University, Maureen Bracewell and Cassandra Bill.

My friend and colleague Dr. Thomas (Tad) McIlwraith (now at University of Guelph) has offered considerable constructive feedback and has been a fabulous sounding board for my thoughts about this book. His many years working with and teaching about First Nations have immense value to me. In particular, I am indebted to Tad for discussions about the nature of First Nations and anthropology in recent times, First Nations in rural and remote areas, and maintaining First Nations identity in the twenty-first century.

I would like to thank Lawrence Paul Yuxweluptun, Matthew Chursinoff, Gillian Crowther, Thomas McIlwraith, Nadine Ryan, and Suzanne Villeneuve, who have let me reproduce their art and photos, as well as those whose images appear in the photos. All are identified in the captions. I owe special acknowledgment to Sonny Assu for letting me reproduce images of several of his art pieces.

I am also grateful to UBC Press for publishing this book. I was under the impression that a book like this would be a hard sell, but when I proposed the first edition to UBC Press, director Peter Milroy and editor Jean Wilson took a risk and let me write the book I wanted, even when some academic peer reviewers suggested otherwise. I am appreciative of that. Both Peter and Jean are now retired, but working under the guidance of current UBC Press acquisitions editor Darcy Cullen and production editor Ann Macklem has been an equally pleasant experience. I also appreciate the excellent suggestions and copy editing of Sarah Wight, and the work of the proofreaders and designers who make me appear to be a better writer than I really am.

While all the people mentioned in these acknowledgments have been important in the writing of this book, their identification here does not necessarily mean they endorse it in its entirety or specific parts. The choice of what to include, and how to include it, remains my responsibility.

Preface

For this third edition of *The First Nations of British Columbia*, the book's primary objective remains unchanged. This book is for readers who would like a fundamental understanding of First Nations peoples, cultures, and issues in the province. Like the previous editions, the book uses a basic anthropological framework to cover the First Nations peoples and cultures of the past and present. It clarifies terminology, includes basic data, covers the ten thousand years before the influence of Europeans, provides an overview of traditional lifeways, describes the impact of Europeans through the nineteenth and twentieth centuries, and discusses the realities of First Nations lives and issues today. This rewritten edition includes totally new introductory and concluding parts, box features, new appendices, updated information and references, and many new illustrations.

First Nations peoples and cultures are a highly visible and important part of the fabric of contemporary British Columbia. Yet, misunderstandings and a general lack of knowledge about First Nations remain among many British Columbians and visitors to the province. This book seeks to address this lack of understanding by filling a niche between media stories and books for the popular or tourist markets on one side and scholarly publications and government reports on the other side. It provides more background and context for understanding the people, the diversity and complexity of cultures, and the issues than media stories can reasonably provide or books largely meant for the popular or tourist market can cover. The book also makes accessible important information gleaned from publications written by academics and those working for provincial and federal governments. This book is written for the generally educated reader, whether academic or non-academic. University or college courses with a specific focus on First Nations of British Columbia are likely to use it as a jumping-off point to delve into information, themes, or issues from more scholarly perspectives. It may also be used as a supplementary textbook to provide background in courses that deal with specific aspects of First Nations peoples or culture. Professionals outside the academic world who deal with specific issues relating to First Nations, including such diverse areas as business, health, law, media, education, and the arts, may find the book valuable for the context it provides. Mostly, though, this book is designed for those who simply want to become more informed about the First Nations peoples and cultures of British Columbia, for reasons including (1) clarifying some complexities and reducing confusion about First Nations peoples, cultures, and issues, (2) wanting better context for understanding current events involving First Nations, and (3) contextualizing an area in which they already have an interest, such as art, history, or business.

The book provides a relatively normative anthropological approach to the study of First Nations. Not all anthropologists would necessarily cover the First Nations of British Columbia in the way they are covered in this book, but there is nothing radical about the coverage.

The book is written from the perspective and based on the experiences of an anthropologist with a passion for postsecondary and public education, all things anthropological, and a special interest in the First Nations of British Columbia. For more than twenty years, I have practised anthropology on behalf of dozens of First Nations in the province, and developed and taught postsecondary courses on First Nations at a variety of BC colleges, institutes, and universities. Many of the First Nations people I have met through my research and teaching have become friends. However, as a middle-aged male of European descent – a third-generation member of the settler or newcomer society – I make no claim of offering an insider's view of First Nations peoples' lives and cultures. My view is that of an anthropologist informed by many years of studying, working with, and interacting with First Nations peoples in both their home communities and educational settings.

A Note about Classification, Territories, Spelling, and Terminology

Not everyone will agree with the classifications, territories, and spelling used in this book. The classification of First Nations is problematic for a variety of reasons, and there is no consensus on which member groups may constitute a distinct First Nation or larger grouping. Nor is there always agreement on the demarcation of traditional territories or the spellings of names and places. The classifications, boundaries, and spellings used here tend to reflect recent research, but are subject to debate and change.

Vocabulary dealing with First Nations and anthropology can be confusing. Readers may come across words that they are unfamiliar with or see words used in unfamiliar ways. To help alleviate confusion, the book includes a glossary. Words in the glossary appear in bold in the text the first time they figure in a main discussion.

Part 1

Introducing First Nations, Popular Perceptions, and the Anthropological Perspective

Popular Perceptions

Popular perceptions of **First Nations** in British Columbia vary immensely and depend very much on context. For many British Columbians as well as visitors to the province, art is what usually first comes to mind when thinking of First Nations. Totem poles and other forms of First Nations art are central themes of tourism marketing campaigns. First Nations public art abounds, including many kinds of art welcoming travellers at Vancouver International Airport, many placements of totem poles in public spaces throughout the province, and public displays in and around many museums, such as the Royal British Columbia Museum and the Museum of Anthropology at the University of British Columbia. Of course, there are countless places selling First Nations tourist art, or kitsch, as well as galleries for connoisseurs of fine art and investors. The images in this part show art ranging from the historical and traditional styles used in totem poles and Bill Reid's sculptures to more modern, explicitly political works by Lawrence Paul Yuxweluptun and Sonny Assu.

Totem Poles

For many, totem poles are a symbol of First Nations in British Columbia. They are a common form of public art throughout the province, images of totems adorn many tourism ads, and miniatures (often manufactured outside the province) are a popular souvenir. Old totems remain, both fallen and standing, in First Nations communities up and down the coast, and new poles continue to be carved and raised as part of tourist attractions, at shopping malls and corporate offices, for museums and reconstructed heritage villages, as public art, and in First Nations communities. Although totem poles are now raised in many areas, traditionally they were restricted to coastal areas. The carving and raising of poles likely goes back thousands of years.

Totem poles in British Columbia can be defined as large wooden poles, usually cedar, carved with images of animate beings. Some define totem poles to include a wide variety of wooden sculptures that may be attached to, or part of the actual structure of, buildings: items sometimes known as house poles or frontal poles, carved planks, grave figures, and welcome figures. A more narrow definition restricts them to free-standing carved poles.

Totem poles are primarily heraldic, rather than depicting gods or being objects of worship themselves. They often depict the crests of kinship groups, or a person's or group's encounter with a supernatural being. The images sometimes involve a transformation with characteristics of both human and animal forms.

As in other kinds of coastal First Nations art, the animals are depicted with certain identifying characteristics. Raven, for example, is always depicted with a straight beak, while Eagle's beak has a downturned tip. Thunderbird often has curled appendages on its head. Bear often has prominent teeth and large clawed feet, Frog has a wide toothless mouth, Wolf has a long snout, and Killer Whale has a dorsal fin.

Traditionally, totem poles were common in the communities of First Nations of the northern and central coastal regions. Poles on the north coast typically had few appendages and rather shallow carving. Poles on the central coast, on the other hand, often were deeply carved with pronounced features, and widely flaring wings were attached. The **Coast Salish** peoples, including those in the southwest portion of the province near Vancouver and surrounding areas, did not traditionally carve free-standing poles, although they produced many other forms of wood sculpture.

Because totem poles were not carved simply for aesthetic reasons, their full meaning is often lost outside of the First Nations culture that created them. Totem poles are intricately linked with other aspects of First Nations cultures: they commemorate important events and people, document histories, validate political and social positions, visualize myths, and assert rights and identity. Replicas made for mass-market sale as tourist items and images used by non-First Nations businesses raise concerns about authenticity and **cultural appropriation** for some First Nations.

Counterclockwise, from top:

Totem poles are among the most visible and well-known representations of First Nations of British Columbia, often used to promote tourism and situated in public places. This is the top of one of several totem poles in Vancouver's Stanley Park, and depicts Thunderbird. Although carvers were traditionally male, this pole was originally carved by Kwakwaka'wakw member Ellen Neel in the 1950s and later refurbished by her son Robert Neel. *Courtesy of Matthew Chursinoff*

The Spirit of Haida Gwaii: The Jade Canoe. This sculpture by Bill Reid is located at the Vancouver airport. Public displays of First Nations art are common within and beyond the borders of British Columbia. This sculpture is a different casting of *The Spirit of Haida Gwaii: The Black Canoe,* which sits outside the Canadian embassy in Washington, DC. *Courtesy of Gillian Crowther*

The Raven and the First Men. This sculpture by Bill Reid illustrates a Haida origin myth. Carved in yellow cedar and on display at the Museum of Anthropology at the University of British Columbia, the sculpture tells the story of how Raven, a prominent character in First Nations myths, coaxed the first Haida out of a giant clamshell. *Photo by Jessica Bushey. Nb1.481, courtesy of UBC Museum of Anthropology, Vancouver, Canada*

Scorched Earth, Clear-Cut Logging on Native Sovereign Land. Shaman Coming to Fix. Painting by Lawrence Paul Yuxweluptun (1991). *Reproduced with the permission of the artist and the National Gallery of Canada*

Breakfast Series, 2006. A series of cereal boxes by Sonny Assu, reflecting a fusion of traditional First Nations design with popular culture and clever commentary on colonialism. *Image courtesy of the artist and the Equinox Gallery.* © *Sonny Assu. Photo by Chris Meier*

It isn't uncommon for First Nations to be characterized by stereotypes. Popular negative stereotypes include the drunken Indian, the lazy Indian, the violent Indian, and the noble savage. Other stereotypes include whiners, complainers, the rich Indian, and the corporate Indian. As most people know, or should know, stereotypes are a dangerous thing, especially stereotypes based on ignorance and misconceptions. Such perceptions of First Nations are often perpetuated by people, corporations, and governments with ulterior motives. For example, governments may benefit from negative stereotypes that perpetuate a culture of dependency by First Nations on government. Similarly, organizations in resource development may benefit from stereotypes of First Nations as impediments to progress.

The Imaginary Indian, the Textbook Indian, and Chief Dan George

A considerable scholarly literature exists on the images of the Native peoples of North America, including the First Nations of British Columbia. *The Imaginary Indian: The Image of the Indian in Canadian Culture,* by Daniel Francis (2nd ed., Vancouver: Arsenal Pulp Press, 2011) outlines several popular perceptions, images, and stereotypes: the noble savage, the vanishing Indian, performing Indians, celebrity Indians, aggressive and bloodthirsty Indians, the spiritual Indian, the environmental Indian, and the cigar store Indian. To these can be added the lazy Indian, the drunken Indian, the angry Indian, and many more, including the relatively recent corporate Indian.

These stereotypes and images are constructed and maintained largely by non-First Nations people, sometimes simply through ignorance, but often with self-interested motives. As motives change, so do the popular stereotypes. In the early years of European interaction with First Nations, such as during the fur trade, the stereotypes and images were usually positive; First Nations people were accommodating hosts, excellent traders, and noble. When people of European descent began coming to British Columbia in significant numbers to seek gold and lands to settle, goals for which First Nations were largely viewed as a hindrance, the stereotypes began to turn negative, in a sense rationalizing the appropriation of lands and resources from the First Nations.

Relatively few British Columbians learn much about First Nations in their schooling. When First Nations are included in the curriculum, stereotypes often remain the norm. In recent years, many British Columbians have been asking why they were not made aware of the atrocities of the **residential school** system, for example. It is an excellent question.

In an article called "Colonizing Minds: Public Education, the 'Textbook Indian,' and Settler Colonialism in British Columbia, 1920-1970" (*BC Studies* 169 [2011]: 101-30), Sean Carleton addresses the representation of First Nations in BC school curriculum. He states, "Authorized textbooks were one tool used by the state to school children in the logic and legitimacy of settler colonialism" (109). The article illustrates how First Nations have been depicted as animal-like, inferior to Europeans, and having a violent disposition, images that reinforce government policies of assimilation and separation to **reserves.**

Carleton identifies Chief Dan George, a member of the Tsleil-Waututh Nation and well-known activist and actor, as among the first to challenge racist stereotyping and textbooks as an important source of colonial power. As part of a celebration of the hundredth anniversary of Canadian Confederation in 1967, Chief Dan George spoke a "Lament for Confederation" that said, in part: "Oh Canada, I am sad for all the Indian people throughout the land ... When I fought to protect my land and my home, I was called a savage. When I was neither understood nor welcomed his way of life, I was called lazy ... My nation was ignored in your history textbooks" (101).

Fortunately, there have been improvements in recent years. The BC Ministry of Education now provides some good resources for educators, and has published a secondary school textbook called *B.C. First Nations Studies* by Kenneth Campbell, Charles Menzies, and Brent Peacock (Victoria: BC Ministry of Education, 2003). But based on the stereotypes and images still perpetuated among many non-First Nations people, there remains a long way to go.

Misconceptions about First Nations peoples and **cultures** are also common. Popular misconceptions are that all First Nations people receive free housing and postsecondary education, and don't have to pay taxes. Other common perceptions are that First Nation cultures are inferior to Euro-Canadian ways, that people of European descent know what is best for First Nations, that with the adoption of modern technologies First Nations cultures cease to exist, and that although First Nations may claim they are trying to protect their land and resources, what they really want is money. The short answers are no, not all First Nations people receive free housing, free postsecondary education, and tax exemptions; First Nations cultures are in no way inferior to other cultures; people of European descent do not necessarily know what is best for First Nations; First Nations cultures remain distinct, even with the adoption of modern technology; and First Nations seeking to protect lands and resources are usually sincere.

Through the Lens of Anthropology
This book has an explicitly anthropological perspective. It draws on information from First Nations, provincial and federal governments, and other academic disciplines, but at its core, it is anthropological. **Anthropology** is the organizing framework used here to choose, describe, and discuss information from various sources. The book is structured around key areas of anthropological interest such as **prehistory**, traditional lifeways, languages, the processes and repercussions of **colonialism**, assertions of rights, and cultural appropriation.

An anthropological perspective also means that a few basic premises underlie the work, namely that (1) understanding contemporary cultures is dependent on knowing their past, (2) all aspects of culture are related, meaning that a change in one element of culture will inevitably cause changes in other aspects of cultures as well, and (3) there are multiple ways of adapting to circumstances and no one way is necessarily better than another. In other words, (1) a good understanding of contemporary First Nations peoples, cultures, and issues is dependent on knowledge of those cultures over the past several thousand years, (2) First Nations technology, diet, economic systems, social and political structures, ideology, and art are all intricately connected, and (3) European and Euro-Canadian ways are not necessarily what is best for First Nations.

Anthropology is broadly defined as the study of humans. This includes humans of the past as well as the present, and it includes the study of both human cultures and human biology. A core concept in anthropology is culture, which may be defined as the learned and shared things that people have, think, and do. The things that people have are physical, such as houses, clothes, tools, and jewellery. The things that people think are commonly referred to as ideology, and include beliefs, values, and morals. The things that people do are what many consider customs or behaviour.

All societies have culture. Major components of culture include subsistence, settlement patterns, technology, communication, economic systems, social systems, political systems, ideology, and art. In British Columbia today, there are many distinct First Nations cultures, most easily inferred by different languages, but also by differences in other elements of culture as well.

One important thing to know about cultures is that things, ideas, and behaviours are constantly changing, because no culture evolves in isolation. Core structures, ideology, and other aspects often remain central, however, meaning that First Nations can adopt technologies, behaviours, and ideologies from other people and still maintain their First Nation culture. This is explored more fully in Part 6.

The four main branches of anthropology are **archaeology, cultural anthropology, linguistic anthropology,** and **biological anthropology.** In British Columbia, archaeology is primarily focused on documenting the physical evidence of human activities in the region before the arrival of Europeans in the late eighteenth and early nineteenth centuries. The nature of archaeology and the results of archaeological research are the focus of Part 3. Cultural anthropology focuses on traditional lifeways and contemporary cultures. Linguistic anthropology involves the study of languages, and biological anthropology is the study of human biological characteristics.

Anthropology emerged as a professional discipline globally in the 1800s, and British Columbia became a focus of attention for many anthropologists in the late 1800s and early 1900s. Some came primarily to collect **artifacts** for museums and private collections, which is why some of the finest examples of First Nations objects are in the British Museum in London, the American Museum of Natural History in New York, the Field Museum in Chicago, the Smithsonian Institution in Washington, DC, and other museums around the world.

During the late 1800s and early 1900s British Columbia became what some have referred to as the most "anthropologized" area of the world. Whether the area does indeed qualify as one of the most anthropologized areas is subject to debate, but substantial research was certainly undertaken. Since the area was the last in North America to have been directly influenced by Europeans, many anthropologists studied the First Nations under the guise of what is known as **salvage ethnography.** Some anthropologists were specialized in one of the major subfields, but many were generalists. It was not uncommon, for example, for anthropologists to immerse themselves in a First Nation, learn the language, document traditional lifeways as described to them by people in the community, excavate **archaeological sites**, and measure the physical characteristics of individuals. In addition to collecting artifacts for museums, some anthropologists also excavated and collected human skeletal remains, and arranged for some First Nations people themselves to travel to Europe and fairs in the United States as a kind of living museum exhibit.

Despite some exceptions, relations between First Nations and anthropologists during the past 150 years have been reasonably good overall. However, anthropology has been criticized as part of the colonialism that has been detrimental to First Nations, and many First Nations people throughout North America had little use for anthropologists. This feeling was articulated most eloquently by Native American scholar Vine Deloria Jr. in a 1969 piece called "Anthropologists and Other Friends," of which the following is a short excerpt:

Into each life, it is said, some rain must fall ... But Indians have been cursed above all other people in history. Indians have anthropologists ... The massive volume of useless knowledge produced by anthropologists ... has contributed substantially to the invisibility of Indian people today ... it would be wise for anthropologists to get down from their thrones of authority and PURE research and begin helping Indian tribes instead of preying on them.

Around the same time, Native American musician and activist Floyd Red Crow Westerman recorded a song called "Here Come the Anthros," which included the lyrics

And the Anthros still keep on coming
Like Death and Taxes to Our Land;
To study their feathered freaks
With funded money in their hand.

Overview of the Book

Part 2 brings some clarification to the often confusing terminology associated with First Nations in the province. A key theme is what constitutes First Nation identity. The part distinguishes the meaning of labels such as **Aboriginal, Indian, Indigenous**; provides basic data on population and reserves; and puts the First Nations of British Columbia into the larger context of Indigenous peoples in Canada, across North America, and globally.

Part 3 focuses on the nature of archaeological research in British Columbia and the conclusions that can be drawn from 50,000 recorded archaeological sites and millions of known artifacts spanning the last 10,000 years or more in the province. The part also includes sections on the legislation governing archaeology, some of the most significant sites, and tracing ancestry through archaeological sites, artifacts, and DNA.

Life immediately before the arrival of Europeans in the region is the focus of Part 4. The core elements of culture, sometimes known as traditional lifeways, are described as they are known or assumed to have existed in the late 1700s. The descriptions include general overviews of the cultures in three major regions of the province – the coastal area, the southern interior, and the northern interior. The part also covers estimates of the First Nations population prior to the arrival of Europeans and the diversity of First Nations languages.

Part 5 covers the period from the late 1700s to the end of the twentieth century, focusing on the impacts of fur traders, gold seekers, missionaries, settlers, and government officials on First Nations peoples and cultures. The part also includes sections on residential schools; government policies, practices, and acts; resistance by First Nations; major court challenges, the beginning of modern treaty negotiations, and the nature of anthropological research in the late twentieth century.

First Nations in the twenty-first century are the focus of Part 6. Sections include an overview of some of the basic realities of contemporary First Nations life (as reflected in census and survey data); modern treaty negotiations; economic and cultural initiatives; major issues within First Nation communities and between First Nations and non-First Nations populations; and the nature of current anthropological work with First Nations.

Recommended Readings and Resources
For more information on totem poles, the following are recommended: *Totem Poles: An Illustrated Guide*, by Marjorie Halpin (Vancouver: UBC Press and the UBC Museum of Anthropology, 1981), *The Totem Poles of Stanley Park*, by Vickie Jensen (Vancouver: Westcoast Words, 2009), *The Totem Pole: An Intercultural History* by Aldona Jonaitis and Aaron Glass (Vancouver: Douglas and McIntyre, 2010), and *Totem Poles*, by Hilary Stewart (Vancouver: Douglas and McIntyre, 1990).

Good books on perceptions, stereotypes, and images of Indigenous peoples in North America include *The Imaginary Indian: The Image of the Indian in Canadian Culture*, by Daniel Francis (2nd ed., Vancouver: Arsenal Pulp Press, 2011), *Playing Indian* by Philip Deloria (New Haven, CT: Yale University Press, 1998), and *The White Man's Indian: Images of the American Indian from Columbus to the Present*, by Robert Berkhofer Jr. (New York: Vintage, 1978). Sean Carleton's "Colonizing Minds: Public Education, the 'Textbook Indian,' and Settler Colonialism in British Columbia, 1920-1970" is in *BC Studies* 169 (2011), 101-30. *B.C. First Nations Studies*, by Kenneth Campbell, Charles Menzies, and Brent Peacock (Victoria: BC Ministry of Education, 2003) is a secondary school textbook.

Vine Deloria Jr. is perhaps the best-known Indigenous critic of anthropology. His piece "Anthropologists and Other

Friends" is a chapter in *Custer Died for Your Sins: An Indian Manifesto*, first published in 1969 (Norman: University of Oklahoma Press).

Part 2

Defining and Situating
First Nations Today

Understanding Labels: First Nations, Aboriginal, Indian, and More

In British Columbia there is general agreement that the term "First Nation" refers to a group of people who can trace their ancestry to the populations that occupied the land before the arrival of Europeans and Americans in the late eighteenth century. Nomenclature for such groups, however, depends on context. Although they were commonly referred to as "nations" from the late eighteenth to the early twentieth centuries, in recent decades they have routinely been referred to as "Indians," "Indian **bands**," "Natives," "Aboriginal peoples," and "Indigenous peoples." "First Nations" customarily describes groups formerly, or also, known as "bands" (the Squamish Band, for example, became the Squamish Nation) as well as affiliations of distinct groups (the Sto:lo Nation, for example, comprises more than a dozen separate, smaller nations). In some situations the community itself may be referred to as a First Nation. The term "First Nation," although used to some extent throughout Canada, is most common in British Columbia.

Proponents of the descriptor "First Nation" cite several benefits. First, it alleviates the derogatory and primitive connotations often associated with the other terms listed above. Second, it corrects the misnomer of "Indians," which resulted from Christopher Columbus's mistaken belief that he had reached India. Third, it emphasizes that the ancestors of today's First Nations people were in the regions prior to the arrival of Europeans. The word "nation" reflects original sovereignty, and its plural, "nations," accentuates the multitude of distinct groups.

Although "First Nations" is increasingly common, it has not totally displaced other terms. "Indian," "Aboriginal," and "band" have specific legal meaning – as described in the Canadian Constitution and the **Indian Act** – and are still widely used by the provincial and federal governments. Some people with ancestral ties to prehistoric populations in the area reject "First Nation" as another label applied by Euro-Canadian society, instead describing their groups with names from their own languages or using such terms as "people," "council," "community," or "village."

Two broad categories of First Nations people live in British Columbia: registered (or status) Indians, and non-status Indians. The terms "registered" and "status" are used interchangeably to distinguish a person whose name appears on a register maintained by the federal government. The criteria for being recognized as a registered Indian have been revised several times by the federal government, with eligibility including such things as ancestry, marriage, education, and occupation.

While most registered Indians have ancestral ties with prehistoric populations, biological relationships have not been necessary to achieve status. For many years, for example, a non-First Nations woman could obtain status by marrying a registered Indian man. Conversely, a person with clear biological ties to prehistoric populations may not necessarily be registered. In the past, status was lost if a registered Indian woman married a non-Indian man. Status could also be lost if a registered Indian obtained a university education, joined the armed forces, or became a Canadian citizen. Some who met the eligibility requirements may simply have been missed during the registration process or chosen to avoid it.

Being registered brings many benefits, especially for those working and living on a reserve. Registered Indians do not pay tax on income earned while working on a reserve or sales taxes on goods purchased on a reserve. Other benefits include comprehensive medical coverage and support for housing and education. Housing and money for education is not unlimited, however, and each First Nation usually determines its members' eligibility for them.

In 1985 the federal government passed Bill C-31, which enabled those who had lost their status, and their descendants, to become registered. At the same time, the federal government legislated that each First Nation would be allowed to create and maintain its own "band list" of members using its own criteria for establishing membership. As a result, it is now possible for a registered Indian to have no affiliation with a specific First Nation, and for a non-status person to be a member of a First Nation.

Population, Reserves, Settlements, and Lands

Approximately 140,000 status and 60,000 non-status Indians live in British Columbia. These figures account for about 5 percent of the total population of the province and about 17 percent of the total First Nations population of Canada.

About 45 percent of the registered Indian population lives on one of the more than 1,500 reserves in the province. The reserves range in size from less than one to more than 18,000 hectares, total about 3,500 square kilometres, and account for less than 1 percent of the land in the province. The majority of reserves are uninhabited. Most of those living on reserves reside in one of about 350 settlements, with an average population between 100 and 200 people. Approximately one-third of the people living on reserves are not registered Indians; usually, these are non-Indigenous people who reside on reserve lands through lease arrangements with the appropriate First Nation.

Lease arrangements with First Nations have also resulted in many businesses locating on reserves. Many First Nations also operate businesses on reserves. Consequently, reserves support a wide variety of commercial enterprises, including marinas, shopping centres, resorts, and wineries.

As a result of recent and ongoing treaty negotiations, the ownership of some reserves, along with other Crown lands, has been transferred to First Nations from the federal

First Nations Identity

First Nations identity can be complex and confusing. On one level, First Nations identity can be personal. Someone may identify as First Nation (or Indian or Aboriginal) as a matter of choice, and not be a member of a specific First Nation or band. Or a First Nation person may have strong biological ties and be registered with the federal government, but choose to not identify as First Nation.

One arbiter of First Nations identity is the federal government. People who meet specific government criteria are registered as "Indian." But being registered or not registered is not necessarily an indicator of **blood quantum**. Many non-status Indians have strong biological ties to ancestral populations, and many registered Indians have no biological ties to ancestral populations at all.

At a First Nation or band level, recognition of membership is usually left to the nation. First Nations commonly create their own membership criteria and maintain their own membership lists. First Nation members are usually also registered Indians, but this is not always the case. It is possible to be a member of a First Nation without being a registered Indian, and it is also possible to be a registered Indian without membership in a specific First Nation or band.

The primary identification for a First Nations person may be with a specific kinship group, community, or reserve. A First Nations person may publicly identify himself or herself as belonging to a specific kin group, a specific community, a specific nation or band, and a specific ethnic group.

In contemporary British Columbia, First Nations (or bands) do not always accurately reflect traditional groupings. Many First Nations/bands in British Columbia are largely the result of decisions made by colonial administrators. Moreover, collective identities and affiliations continue to shift as nations split and amalgamate. It has become common for representatives of multiple First Nations ethnic groups to be members of a single First Nation or band.

Many First Nations people challenge the labels "Aboriginal" or "Indian," which were created by Euro-Canadians. Similarly, "First Nations" is also often rejected because it is less meaningful than the name of their own community or kin group.

government. These are frequently referred to as "band lands" or lands belonging to a specific nation. For example, close to 2,000 square kilometres in the Nass River area of northeastern British Columbia now belong to the Nisga'a Nation and are widely known as Nisga'a Lands.

Bands, Ethnic Groups, Tribal Councils, and Other Affiliations

For most registered Indians, the primary unit of administration is the band. As defined by the Indian Act, "band" means "a body of Indians ... for whose use and benefit in common, lands, the legal title to which is vested in Her Majesty, have been set apart." The governance of most bands follows the Indian Act, which calls for an elected chief and council, with the number of councillors dependent on the number of band members: one councillor for every hundred members, with a minimum of two and a maximum of twelve.

Reserves, and most funds from the federal government destined for the registered Indian population, tend to be allocated to bands. The bands are therefore the most direct channel for First Nations people to obtain their benefits and entitlements as registered Indians.

In many cases bands do not reflect past social and political organization. In the nineteenth century the federal government created bands largely for its own benefit, to make it easier to administer and control First Nations. Due to a lack of understanding by Euro-Canadians, some traditional groupings were deemed to be separate bands, while in other cases distinct groups were amalgamated to form a single band. In the past the federal government has also arbitrarily declared some bands extinct.

The creation of new bands through amalgamation in the early twentieth century was also often for the benefit of the federal government, in the form of administrative efficiency, particularly as First Nations populations were declining.

Where Do First Nations People Live in British Columbia?

About 200,000 First Nations people live in British Columbia, including both registered and non-status Indians. About one-third of the total First Nations population lives on reserves. The overwhelming majority of off-reserve First Nations people (81 percent) live in urban areas. Urban areas with the highest numbers of First Nations people, starting with the most populous, are Vancouver, Victoria, Prince George, Kelowna, Abbotsford, Kamloops, Nanaimo, Prince Rupert, Chilliwack, Campbell River, Terrace, Duncan, Port Alberni, Vernon, Courtney, Williams Lake, Fort St. John, Dawson Creek, Burns Lake, Quesnel, Penticton, Merritt, and Cranbrook.

More than half of the First Nations populations live in southwestern British Columbia, with the highest numbers in the Vancouver area, the Fraser Valley, and southern Vancouver Island, mirroring the distribution of the BC population as a whole. The northern regions of the province have the highest percentages of First Nations people within their populations, especially in the central and northern coastal regions. For example, First Nations people account for more than 60 percent of the central coastal region's population. For comparison, First Nations people represent about 15 percent of the population in the Cariboo, about 12 percent in the Peace River and Squamish-Lillooet areas, about 6 percent in the Fraser Valley, Powell River, and the Sunshine Coast, about 4 percent in the Okanagan and Kootenays, and about 2 percent in Greater Vancouver.

Recent creation of new bands, however, has most often been at the request of First Nations, usually reflecting more traditional groupings or more efficient administration.

Depending on how one defines a nation, there may be as few as ten or more than 200 First Nations in the province. There are about 200 bands based in British Columbia (see Appendix 1) as well as a few bands based in the Yukon and

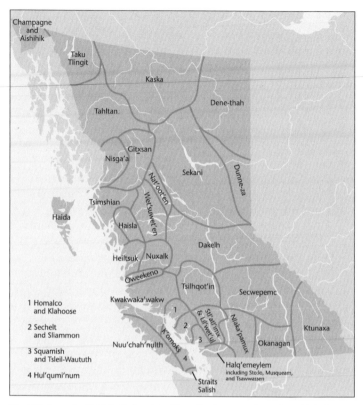

First Nations in British Columbia. First Nations are largely self-defined. Identified here are the major ethnic groups, based on shared territory, language, and culture. Some ethnic groups are represented by a single First Nation; others comprise multiple smaller First Nations, sometimes known as bands.

Northwest Territories that claim part of British Columbia as their traditional territory. For those who believe that a band equates with a nation, there are therefore about 200 First Nations in the province.

Historically, bands were commonly divided into ten major groupings: Haida, Tsimshian, Kwakiutl, Nootka, Coast Salish, **Interior Salish**, Bella Coola, Athapaskan, Inland Tlingit, and Kutenai. Although these groupings are an overly simplistic

Coke Salish, 2006. By Sonny Assu. *Image courtesy of the artist and the Equinox Gallery.* © *Sonny Assu. Photo by Chris Meier*

and largely inaccurate way to describe the diversity of First Nations in British Columbia, they unfortunately remain widely used.

It is now commonly held that there are thirty to forty major ethnic groups among First Nations in British Columbia today (see the map on the facing page, and Appendix 2). The criteria for distinguishing the groups include shared territory, language, and culture. Most of these ethnic groups have further subdivisions – such as nation, community, or family group – to which individuals have a stronger bond.

Some categories or classifications, such as Coast Salish and Interior Salish, represent neither a distinct culture nor a language. Rather, such categories represent a number of different nations and ethnic groups that have similar, but still distinct, cultures and languages. Coast Salish, for example, may refer to members of the Halq'emeylem (including Sto:lo, Musqueam, and Tsawwassen), Sechelt, Squamish, and Tsleil-Waututh nations.

The distinctions between and mapping of major ethnic groups are constantly changing. First Nations people and anthropologists, often in association with each other, are continually working to clarify traditional groupings and territories, but there are many problems: historical records offer contradictory information, Euro-Canadians have often misunderstood languages and organizations, many First Nations have been known by a variety of names and disagree among themselves about terminology, and there are no consistent criteria for distinguishing the groups. As a result, there is no consensus on the number and names of major ethnic groups, let alone on territorial boundaries.

Similarly, identification of the specific nations that belong to the larger ethnic groups is problematic, largely because communities have changed as the boundaries of traditional territories have altered and populations have mixed. It is not unusual for nations to be linked with more than one ethnic group.

About 90 percent of First Nations are affiliated with tribal councils, which are associations of bands formed to deal with administrative, economic, political, or other matters. There are currently about thirty tribal councils in the province. They tend to be regional, and although they are usually formed by nations within a single ethnic group, they may cross ethnic boundaries.

First Nations people in British Columbia may have many other affiliations, including to organizations that support arts, economic development, health, education, and politics. Many First Nations have also formed affiliations to negotiate treaties.

Some prominent First Nations organizations are frequently mentioned in media. The British Columbia Assembly of First Nations is the regional branch of the National Assembly of First Nations, which primarily represents the registered Indian population in matters pertaining to national issues.

Community members in button blanket robes. Garments such as button blanket robes typically depict family groups and are often worn for ceremonial occasions, such as shown here in the Haida community of Massett. *Courtesy of Gillian Crowther*

The Union of British Columbia Indian Chiefs represents the interests of some, but not all, registered Indian populations on local, regional, and sometimes national issues. The First Nations Summit focuses primarily on issues of concern to nations involved in treaty-making. The United Native

In Secwepemc territory. Stuart Lee and his son Lucas, from Splatsin, one of about 200 First Nations in the province. They are shown here on a reserve near Enderby. About 45 percent of the registered First Nations population live on one of the approximately 1,500 reserves in the province, mostly in rural areas. *Courtesy of Thomas McIlwraith*

Nations, formerly known as the British Columbia Association of Non-Status Indians, represents the interests of off-reserve First Nations people and Métis.

Situating BC First Nations within Canada, in North America, and around the World

The more than 200,000 people identifying as First Nation in British Columbia are part of the approximately six million people claiming Indigenous ancestry in North America. This total includes all of those categorized as Aboriginal in Canada (i.e., Indians, Inuit, and Métis) and as Native American in the United States (i.e., Indians, Aleut, and Eskimo). The 200 First Nations in British Columbia represent about a third of the registered bands in Canada and 17 percent of the approximately 1,150 federally recognized First Nations and Native American groups.

On a global scale, the United Nations estimates that there are about 370 million Indigenous people in ninety countries. First Nations people in British Columbia are sometimes vocal on the international stage about issues common to Indigenous peoples everywhere, such as the 2007 United Nations Declaration on the Rights of Indigenous Peoples. (Interestingly, the Canadian government was one of only four governments that voted against the declaration, along with the governments of Australia, New Zealand, and the United States, although each subsequently reversed its position and endorsed it.) Because of their similar colonial histories, the First Nations of British Columbia tend to be most closely aligned with Indigenous peoples of Australia, New Zealand, and the United States.

Recommended Readings and Resources
The websites of Aboriginal Affairs and Northern Development Canada (www.aandc-aadnc.gc.ca) and the provincial Ministry of Aboriginal Relations and Reconciliation (www.gov.bc.ca/arr) are both good places to obtain basic data about First Nations, including profiles of each nation. The websites of the British Columbia Assembly of First Nations (www.bcafn.ca), the Union of British Columbia Indian Chiefs (www.ubcic.bc.ca), and the First Nations Summit (www.fns.bc.ca) also provide information about First Nations. Statistics Canada (www.statcan.gc.ca) and BC Stats (www.bcstats.gov.bc.ca) publish data on First Nations people, including reports based on the Canadian census, taken every five years.

Indigenous identity in North America is an area of considerable interest. *The Power of Place, the Problem of Time: Aboriginal Identity and Historical Consciousness in the Cauldron of Colonialism*, by Keith Thor Carlson (Toronto: University of Toronto Press, 2010), covers the shifting nature of cultural and political collective identities among Sto:lo. *Real Indians:*

Identity and the Survival of Native America, by Eva Marie Garroutte (Berkeley: University of California Press, 2003), focuses on the complexities of Indian identity in North America. *Who Is an Indian? Race, Place, and the Politics of Indigeneity in the Americas*, edited by Maximilian Forte (Toronto: University of Toronto Press, 2013), includes contributions on Canadian, American, and Caribbean communities.

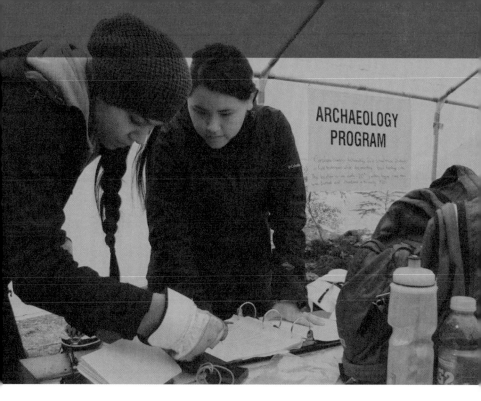

Part 3

Archaeology and First Nations

First Nations and Archaeological Perceptions of the Past

The **myths** of First Nations people in British Columbia often state that they have occupied their traditional territories since "time immemorial" (which can roughly be translated as "forever") with relatively little change in their traditional lifeways over time. Details vary considerably among nations, but the origin stories generally follow a common theme. A creator placed people in their territory, and then either the creator or another supernatural entity provided values, customs, and languages that have since been maintained.

Although they agree that First Nations people have been in the area now known as British Columbia a very long time, archaeologists tell a different story about how and when people first came to this part of the world and what cultural changes they subsequently experienced. Archaeologists state with a high degree of confidence that people have been in the area for at least 11,000 years.

The Nature of Archaeological Research in British Columbia

Archaeological research began in British Columbia during the late nineteenth century with only a handful of professional archaeologists working in the province at any time. Despite a very limited amount of research, a broad outline of the human past in the province was established by the 1960s, including indications of approximately when people first arrived, what they were doing, and the differences in lifeways in various regions.

Although refining culture history – describing archaeological sites, artifacts, and the basic sequence of human events – remains a goal of archaeologists working in the province, the nature of archaeological research changed significantly in the late twentieth century. Prior to the 1960s, archaeology in British Columbia could be characterized as driven by the pursuit of artifacts for museums and the wish to determine

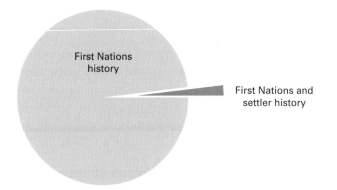

First Nations have been in the province for at least 11,000 years, while Europeans have coexisted with them for barely 200. *Based on a graphic created by Quentin Mackie*

an outline of culture history. Pure archaeological research today, such as that directed by archaeologists working in universities, focuses not only on what people were doing and when they were doing it, but also on why they were doing it and how change occurred.

While pure research interests are important, at least 90 percent of archaeological research in British Columbia in contemporary times has been undertaken in the name of **cultural resource management**, often abbreviated CRM, and also known as commercial archaeology. Essentially, this means that archaeology is done because the provincial government believes a land-altering development project may destroy archaeological sites both known and unknown, and requires the development company to have archaeologists determine the potential impact of the proposed development. Archaeologists then examine the proposed area to look for sites, assess their significance, and make recommendations to the government if sites may potentially be destroyed. In some cases, they excavate significant sites that will be destroyed by development.

During the past few decades much archaeological research has also been undertaken as a result of litigation and negotiation. First Nations, the provincial and federal governments, and corporations have contracted archaeologists to undertake research in preparation for court cases involving **Aboriginal rights,** and in preparation for treaty negotiation. Many First Nations in British Columbia now have their own departments to oversee or carry out archaeological research in their traditional territories. Some have their own permit systems, meaning that in addition to obtaining a permit from the provincial government to undertake archaeological field work, archaeologists must also obtain permission from the First Nation(s) that claims the area as being within its traditional territory. Many First Nations people have pursued careers in archaeology. It is now common for First Nations archaeologists to be doing field work on both commercial and academic-based projects in the province, as well as pursuing advanced degrees.

Archaeological sites in British Columbia are protected by provincial and federal legislation. Many sacred or spiritual sites are not protected, however, because they are not defined as archaeological sites, which requires physical evidence of human activity. The British Columbia Heritage Conservation Act (Appendix 3) makes it illegal for anyone without a permit to disturb an archaeological site not on a reserve or in a national park. This includes private property. Penalties for contravening the act include a fine of up to $50,000 and up to two years in jail for individuals, and a fine of up to $1 million for corporations. A person has to meet stringent requirements in order to get a permit from the provincial government, including a university degree in archaeology or a related discipline and considerable archaeological field experience in the province. Legislation protecting archaeological sites on reserves and national parks (and other federal lands) can be found in the Indian Act, the National Parks Act,

First Nations women doing archaeology. Amanda Vick (Gitxsan name Seemadam) of the Gitxsan Nation and Tiana Lewis of the Squamish Nation doing archaeology on an excavation project. Substantial numbers of First Nations people do archaeology, and many First Nations have their own archaeology or heritage departments. *Courtesy of Nadine Ryan*

the Historic Sites and Monuments Act, and the Canadian Environmental Assessment Act. The Indian Act, for example, makes it illegal to remove pictographs (paintings on rock), petroglyphs (carvings on rock), and carved poles from reserves unless they were specifically manufactured for sale.

The provincial government maintains a record of archaeological sites in British Columbia. The number of sites in the inventory currently sits at about 50,000 and encompasses a wide diversity of types, including prehistoric villages; campsites; burial grounds; places where plants and animals were harvested, processed, or stored; places where raw materials were harvested or transformed into artifacts; and rock art. One of the most common kinds of sites in coastal areas are **middens**, which are usually the trash dumps associated with villages. Middens with a visible component of shell are referred to as shell middens and often extend several thousand years into the past.

Almost all the recorded archaeological sites in the province have been recorded by professional archaeologists over the past several decades. In recent years most have been recorded by archaeologists assessing the potential impact of development projects. Natural processes such as erosion have probably destroyed thousands of sites. Urban development, forestry, mining, pipelines, dams, road building, and other human activities have likely destroyed tens of thousands more.

Early Migrations through British Columbia

Most archaeologists concur that the ancestry of all the Indigenous peoples of North, Central, and South America lies in Asia, and that the route taken from Asia to the Americas was via a land bridge known as **Beringia**, the area surrounding what is now the Bering Strait. Opinion diverges, however,

---

What Constitutes the Archaeological Record?

In common usage, "the archaeological record" refers to all the recorded physical evidence of past human activities in a region, including archaeological sites and artifacts. On a broader level, the archaeological record may also be taken to include all the related documentation, such as field notes, maps, and completed forms, as well as all the reports and articles about the past based on the physical remains. The official keeper of the record in British Columbia is the Archaeology Branch of the provincial government, which archives the archaeological site inventory forms and completed reports for all archaeological projects undertaken with a permit issued by the branch.

An archaeological site can be defined as any location where there is physical evidence of past human activity. Since provincial legislation protects only sites older than AD 1846,

---

most sites on record are older than that. In practice, how archaeologists define an archaeological site depends on the objectives of the project. In some cases, a single artifact may be all that is required to designate a location as an archaeological site, while other cases may require a minimum number of artifacts in an area before site designation. Thus, some sites comprise a single artifact, while other sites contain tens of thousands of artifacts as well as remnants of houses and other aspects of village life spanning several thousand years.

There are several major kinds of archaeological sites. Habitation sites include both villages and temporary camps. A common feature of sites occupied over a significant length of time are middens, which are essentially trash heaps created by the village's occupants. Rock art sites are usually identified as pictographs (rock paintings) and petroglyphs (incising or carving into rock). Culturally modified trees exhibit some kind of modification by First Nations people, such as bark stripping, taking planks out of trees for house construction, or removing blocks for making masks. Resource utilization areas are associated with fishing, hunting, and plant collecting as well as processing and storing foods. One of the most common kinds of sites are lithic scatters, which are essentially the waste that was left behind by someone making stone tools.

Artifacts are portable objects that were made or used by humans, including such things as tools and jewellery. Most of the millions of artifacts recorded in British Columbia are made from stone, but that is at least partly due to preservation. Many thousands of stone spear points, arrowheads, hammerstones, bowls, and beads are part of the archaeological record. Artifacts made of bone, antler, shell, bark, and textiles tend to be less common due to much poorer preservation of organic materials.

It is relatively rare to find a complete artifact. For every complete arrowhead found, there are probably dozens of broken ones. For every artifact that makes it to a display case in a museum, there are probably hundreds of artifacts in storage, interesting and significant to First Nations and archaeologists but lacking popular appeal. The artifacts archaeologists discover were often deliberately discarded as waste.

on the timing of the initial migration into the Americas and the route taken from Beringia areas south of what is now the US-Canadian border. Archaeologists are relatively certain of two things: that people have occupied regions south of what is now Canada for at least 14,000 years, and that movements into those areas involved passing through portions of what is now British Columbia.

While Beringia supported a diverse array of plants and animals, prior to about 11,000 years ago most of what is now British Columbia was under ice. Exceptions include parts of the Pacific coast and part of the northeastern region. Some archaeologists speculate that people may have followed the coast south from Beringia; others maintain that an inland route was more likely. The coastal route would probably have involved short-term occupations of dry land by a maritime-adapted people. The inland route would have involved travel by terrestrial-adapted people through an ice-free corridor from Beringia through northeastern British Columbia and south along the eastern side of the Rocky Mountains. Although most archaeologists are confident that people must have migrated through one or both of these routes between 20,000 and 14,000 years ago, there is no undisputed physical evidence of humans in the province prior to about 11,000 years ago. Environmental evidence indicates that both routes were feasible, because plants and animals were sufficiently abundant and diverse to support human populations.

The lack of evidence of archaeological sites older than 11,000 years in British Columbia has multiple explanations. One is that such sites would have very low archaeological visibility. People migrating along the coast or through the northeastern part of the province would have been unlikely to live in permanent settlements or create large trash areas (i.e., middens) to be identified by archaeologists. Similarly, because the number of people moving through the region was probably small, they probably didn't create many sites.

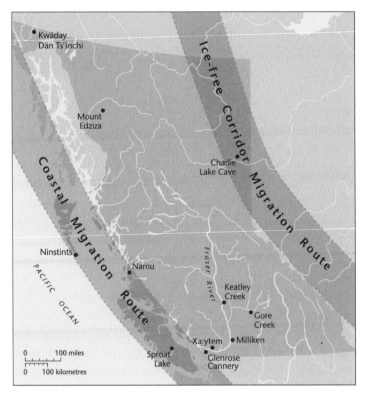

Major archaeological sites and early migration routes in British Columbia. There are approximately 50,000 recorded archaeological sites in the province. During the last ice age, when most of the province was under ice, people occupied and travelled down the coast and may have occupied and travelled through the northeastern part of the province as well.

The preservation of organic remains, such as the remnants of meals or shelters, decreases the farther back in time one goes. Discovering archaeological sites older than 11,000 years is also problematic because sea levels, rivers, lakes, and other landforms have changed significantly since that time. Due largely to glaciers melting, sea levels along the coast of British Columbia rose, likely submerging and perhaps destroying much of the evidence of older sites. Sea levels stabilized at the current levels only about 5,000 years ago. Also, few archaeologists have focused on finding sites in the relatively small areas of British Columbia that were not glaciated prior to 11,000 years ago.

Here to Stay

Environmental and archaeological evidence indicates that by about 11,000 years ago, the glaciers had mostly melted, a wide variety of plants and animals had become established, and people from previously unglaciated portions of North America (such as Alaska, Washington, Oregon, and Montana) were arriving and settling in what is now British Columbia. Groups arriving from the north, the south, and the southeast brought their own distinctive cultures, which can be identified in the archaeological assemblages.

Groups occupying British Columbia between about 11,000 and 5,000 years ago can be characterized as generalized foragers, typically living in nomadic bands of thirty to fifty people and utilizing a wide variety of resources. Archaeological sites reflect a pattern of temporary settlements, with no permanent structures, although many sites were utilized many times, probably on an annual basis. Along with some plants and terrestrial animals, fish and sea mammals were important resources for people living in coastal areas. Some people in interior regions also ate fish, but it was not as important to their diet as it was for coastal peoples. People of the interior relied more on terrestrial resources, including big game animals. Population densities were relatively low during this period, although people were aware of, and interacted with, other groups. There were multiple ethnic groups (each with its own language), with multiple bands (groups) in each.

Settling Down

The cultures of many groups underwent significant change between 5,000 and 3,000 years ago. The unique and sophisticated lifeways exhibited by First Nations of the coastal region, as witnessed by the first Europeans to the area and continuing in some forms today, can be traced to this period (and sometimes earlier). These include large winter villages with large houses constructed from cedar planks, a significant dependence on salmon and other marine resources in the diet, highly developed stone and plant technologies, complex social and political structures, and distinctive art. Similar lifeways among groups residing in the southern interior can also be traced to this period.

The changes for both coastal and southern interior groups were probably triggered by the ability to harvest salmon in abundant quantities. This may have resulted from natural processes, such as the stabilization of sea levels and river systems leading to increased numbers and productivity of salmon, or from cultural processes, such as the development of more efficient salmon harvesting, processing, or storage technologies. The abundance of salmon was such that peoples where salmon were widely available (i.e., in coastal areas and along river systems travelled by salmon) had enough surplus food to support or lead to higher populations, the development of large winter villages and houses, sophisticated technologies, increased social stratification, complex ceremonies, and sophisticated art. Groups of these times and places are often referred to by archaeologists and other anthropologists as specialized foragers or complex foragers.

Prominent Sites
Prominent early archaeological sites in the northern interior regions of British Columbia include Charlie Lake Cave and Mount Edziza. Located in the northeast, near Fort St. John, Charlie Lake Cave was first excavated in the 1980s. The lower levels of the deposit, which contained tools, bison bones, and jewellery, were radiocarbon dated to almost 11,000 years ago, making Charlie Lake Cave the oldest reliably dated site in the

province. One of the artifacts found was a fluted point, a type of stone spearhead fairly rare in western Canada but commonly found in sites elsewhere in North America and almost always dated to between 12,000 and 9,000 years ago. Fluted points are usually associated with the killing and butchering of bison, mammoths, and mastodons. Thus, Charlie Lake Cave provides evidence of an early occupation of the area, a big-game adaptation, and considerable interaction and mobility of groups across North America, including British Columbia.

Found in many archaeological sites in British Columbia is a kind of fine-grained volcanic rock known as obsidian. The crystalline structure of obsidian gives it excellent flaking properties, and it was therefore prized for use in the manufacture of stone tools. Much of the obsidian in northern areas has been traced to the area around Mount Edziza, near Telegraph Creek in northwestern British Columbia. An archaeological survey of the area found millions of pieces of obsidian that had been modified by humans, suggesting that those visiting the area did some manufacturing of artifacts on-site. Obsidian from Mount Edziza has been used throughout northern British Columbia for the past several thousand years.

Archaeology and Human Remains

The search for and excavation of human burials is a topic of considerable interest in British Columbia. Thousands of human burials have been excavated in the name of archaeology since the late 1800s. One site alone – variously referred to as the Great Fraser Midden, the Marpole Midden, and Čʔəsnaʔəm, in south Vancouver – reportedly had several hundred skeletons removed in the early years of archaeology and specimen collecting for museums.

Although some archaeologists continue to actively search for and excavate human remains in British Columbia for pure research purposes, it would be unusual for such work to be done today without the express permission of local First Nations. When skeletons are uncovered during excavations, archaeologists will accede to the wishes of the First Nation, either leaving the remains in place, excavating the remains for reburial elsewhere by the First Nation, or excavating and analyzing the remains before subsequent reburial or storage. In the case of Kwäday Dän Ts'ìnchi, discussed elsewhere in this chapter, for example, the Champagne and Aishihik First Nations gave permission for archaeologists to study his remains for a specified length of time before he was returned to them.

Some First Nations want archaeologists to search for and examine burial sites. In some cases they wish to assess their condition in view of ongoing environmental and cultural developments. In other cases, First Nations support excavation of burial sites in order to learn more about their past. The Sechelt Nation, for example, recently collaborated on the excavations of some burials in their territory. These burials revealed the existence of remarkable social and political structures thousands of years ago. Associated with one 4,000-year-old burial of a single individual were 350,000 stone and shell beads.

Although much can be learned from skeletal remains and associated burial objects, few archaeologists in British Columbia believe that knowledge is more important than the wishes of the First Nations. When it comes to development, however, developers and the government do not always take this position. First Nations opposition to the disturbance of burials in the name of development tends to garner relatively little popular support. This may be attributed in part to media using the language of archaeology, which is often disconnected from First Nations culture. What archaeologists and media may call a midden, First Nations may view as a burial ground; where archaeologists and media refer to human remains as skeletons, First Nations may call them ancestors; where archaeologists and media may refer to an area as prehistoric, First Nations may call it a village.

Many sites along the central and northern coast provide evidence of at least 10,000 years of occupation. Namu, on the central coast, is a large shell midden site providing a sequence of culture history spanning close to 10,000 years. It is one of the most intensively studied archaeological sites in the province. Excavations during the 1970s, 1980s, and 1990s have provided a wealth of information on coastal prehistory, especially about subsistence.

Several sites in the 7,000-9,000 year range have been discovered in the southern interior of the province. Located near Kamloops, the Gore Creek site contained the remains of a young adult male who died in a mudslide. The mud had preserved the skeleton, but no artifacts were recovered. The skeleton was radiocarbon dated to over 8,000 years, and further testing of the bones indicated that marine protein, probably salmon, was part of his diet.

Several sites of similar age exist in southwest British Columbia, although relatively few early sites have survived the urbanization of the Vancouver area. One that has is the Glenrose Cannery site in Surrey, first excavated in the 1970s, which has provided important information on regional prehistory over the last 9,000 years. The Milliken site, near Yale on the Fraser River, is another important early site that has provided evidence of lifeways in the Fraser Canyon 8,000 or more years ago.

One of the most significant archaeological sites dating to the last few thousand years is the Keatley Creek site, near Lillooet. This is likely the most intensively excavated site in British Columbia, with multiple excavation projects ongoing since the 1980s. Close to 100 houses have been identified in this very large village site. Excavations indicate a highly complex social and political organization.

The significance of archaeological sites in British Columbia is customarily assessed according to their value to archaeolo-

Keatley Creek archaeological site. Archaeologist Brian Hayden and Bob Muckle are near the rim of one of many housepits at the site, while the core of the site is in the background. Brian Hayden has directed most of the research at Keatley Creek since the 1980s. The site includes approximately 100 housepits, which is what is left of a semi-subterranean pithouse after it is abandoned and collapses. A pithouse from a different site is shown on p. 59. *Courtesy of Suzanne Villeneuve*

gists for describing and explaining the past. No less important, however, is their value to First Nations and the public. Rock art, for example, is appealing to everyone, especially if it is easily accessible, and often has spiritual connotations for First Nations. For example, the Sproat Lake petroglyphs on Vancouver Island have significance to First Nations insofar as they both depict and are thought to be the work of mythological beings.

Another site of great significance to First Nations, the public, and archaeology in general is Xa:ytem, also known as the

Sproat Lake petroglyphs. These prehistoric rock carvings, outlined in white for photographic reasons, are located near Port Alberni on Vancouver Island. There are thousands of rock art sites throughout the province. *Courtesy of Royal BC Museum, BC Archives, H-07372*

Hatzic Rock site, located near Mission in the Fraser Valley. Like the Sproat Lake petroglyphs, Xa:ytem has easy access and is thought to have been created by a transformer. Excavations at the site revealed tens of thousands of artifacts and the remains of several houses several thousand years old. The Sto:lo operate an interpretive centre at the site.

Tatshenshini-Alsek Provincial Park, in the extreme northwest corner of the province where Alaska, the Yukon, and British Columbia intersect, is the site of a discovery that has garnered considerable interest among First Nations and archaeologists. In 1999 three hunters discovered the frozen remains of a young adult male and some of his belongings left visible by a melting glacier. Although only hundreds, rather than thousands, of years old, it is probably the oldest body with well-preserved soft tissue in North America. The artifacts found with the body offer contradictory evidence of his homeland. Some artifacts, such as a cedar-woven hat, suggest a coastal home, while a robe made from squirrel suggests the interior. The contents of his stomach and intestines are equally contradictory, suggesting travels in both coastal and inland regions. On his discovery, members of the Champagne and Aishihik First Nations named the individual Kwäday Dän Ts'ìnchi, meaning "long-ago person found."

Internationally, the most well-known archaeological site in the province is likely Ninstints on Anthony Island in Haida Gwaii (formerly Queen Charlotte Islands), also known as SGang Gwaay. The site was a thriving Haida village prior to and immediately following initial contact with Europeans in the late eighteenth century. By the mid-1800s the population had been decimated by smallpox and the village abandoned. Based primarily on the remains of houses and large collection of carved poles at the site, it has been declared a World Heritage Site by UNESCO (United Nations Educational, Scientific, and Cultural Organization). It is one of only a handful of First Nations sites in North America to be afforded this status and the only one in British Columbia.

Tracing Ancestry

For both scholarly and practical reasons, such as support for Aboriginal rights, archaeologists frequently attempt to trace the ancestry of today's First Nations into the prehistoric past. They are confident that direct ancestry for most First Nations can be traced at least a few and in many cases several thousand years back. Migrations of groups into territory previously sparsely occupied have been identified, such as the movement of a group from the northeastern part of the province into the Nicola Valley in the southern interior several hundred years ago. There is little evidence, however, of large-scale migrations of people displacing pre-existing nations. Boundaries between nations have shifted through time, but most nations have probably maintained their core territories for thousands of years.

Tracing the ancestry of populations into the past is usually based on similarities and differences in archaeological sites and artifacts through time in a region. Recent advances in methods have allowed archaeologists and others to add DNA studies to their toolkit. Researchers recently extracted DNA from several prehistoric skeletons and living First Nations people in the north coast region. Results show a link between a 5,500-year-old skeleton, a 2,500-year-old skeleton, and a living member of the Metlakatla First Nation.

Recommended Readings and Resources
Good general overviews of BC prehistory include Roy Carlson's introductory chapter in *The Pacific Province: A History of British Columbia*, edited by Hugh Johnston (Vancouver: Douglas and McIntyre, 1996), and Knut Fladmark's *British Columbia Prehistory* (Ottawa: National Museums of Canada, 1986). Those interested in particular regions or periods may find the following books useful: *Emerging from the Mist: Studies in Northwest Coast Culture History*, edited by R.G. Matson, Gary Coupland, and Quentin Mackie (Vancouver: UBC Press, 2003), *Peoples of the Northwest Coast: Their Archaeology and Prehistory*, by Kenneth M. Ames and Herbert D.G. Maschner (New York: Thames and Hudson, 1999), *Western Subarctic Prehistory*, by Donald W. Clark (Hull, QC: Canadian Museum of Civilization, 1991), *Early Human Occupation of British Columbia*, edited by Roy L. Carlson and Luke Dalla Bona (Vancouver: UBC Press, 1996), *Prehistory of the Northwest Coast*, by R.G. Matson and Gary Coupland (New York: Academic Press, 1994), and *People of the Middle Fraser Canyon: An Archaeological History*, by Anna Marie Prentiss and Ian Kuijt (Vancouver: UBC Press, 2012).

For a critical history of archaeology in the province focusing on the complicity of archaeologists in disassociating

Musqueam people from burial grounds and other lands, see *These Mysterious People: Shaping History and Archaeology in a Northwest Community*, by Susan Roy (Montreal: McGill-Queen's University Press, 2010).

Part 4

Languages, Population Estimates, and Traditional Lifeways

This part provides an overview of the traditional lifeways of First Nations people as they were when Europeans and Americans arrived in the late eighteenth and early nineteenth centuries. Traditional lifeways are sometimes called "precolonial," referring to the time before Vancouver Island was made a British colony in 1849 and the colony of British Columbia was created in 1858. Languages and populations are also discussed.

Information on traditional lifeways comes from multiple sources, including oral histories, ethnographic research, historical documents, and archaeology. Much of the early anthropological work in British Columbia, in the late 1800s and early 1900s, was in the manner of **recall ethnography**. An anthropologist would typically work closely with one or a few members of a community, often elders, who were knowledgeable about the group's past and willing to share. They would tell the anthropologist what they had been told, and what they recalled, about earlier times. The anthropologist would then describe these accounts in book form, called an **ethnography**. Historical documents include the writings of early European visitors to the region, and archaeology provides physical evidence of those lifeways. Oral tradition, ethnographies, historical documents, and archaeology tend to support the same, or at least very similar, accounts of how life was in the late eighteenth and early nineteenth centuries, prior to significant impacts triggered by the arrival of Europeans.

Since the focus of this part is on the lifeways as they were before the arrival of Europeans in the region, much of the writing uses the past tense. It should be understood and appreciated, however, that many elements of traditional lifeways continue to be integral components of First Nations cultures today.

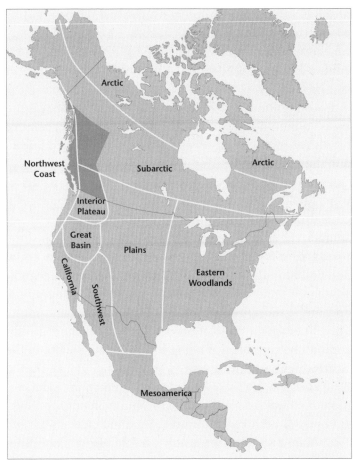

Culture areas of North America. First Nations in each culture area shared similar lifeways. The Northwest Coast, Subarctic, and Interior Plateau are each well represented in British Columbia, and the Ktunaxa of southeastern British Columbia have many similarities with Plains cultures.

Traditional Culture Areas of British Columbia

Culture area is a core anthropological concept used in the study of Indigenous peoples of North America prior to and soon after the arrival of Europeans. Simply defined, a culture area was a geographic region in which separate societies had similar cultures. Many different nations existed in a single culture area, but taken as a group, the lifeways within a single culture area contrasted with the lifeways of nations in other culture areas.

British Columbia includes parts of three of the ten culture areas commonly recognized for the Indigenous peoples of North America: the Northwest Coast, the Interior Plateau, and the Subarctic.

The Northwest Coast encompasses the coastal region from Alaska to northern California. The environment is a coastal rainforest with plentiful marine and terrestrial resources. The cultures of the late prehistoric and early historic periods usually had a marine-based economy, complex social and political organization, and sophisticated wood technology and art. Salmon and cedar were important resources, and the characteristic winter dwelling was a plank house. There was a high population density. Major ethnic groups commonly considered as being within the BC portion of the Northwest Coast culture area include Gitxsan, Haida, Haisla, Halq'emeylem, Heiltsuk, Homalco, Hul'qumi'num, Klahoose, K'omoks, Kwakwaka'wakw, Nisga'a, Nuu'chah'nulth, Nuxalk, Oweekeno, Sechelt, Sliammon, Squamish, Straits Salish, Tsimshian, and Tsleil-Waututh. The Taku Tlingit are sometimes considered as being within the Northwest Coast culture area and sometimes as within the Subarctic.

The Interior Plateau includes the southern interior of British Columbia and the interior portions of the Pacific Northwest states – Washington, Oregon, and Idaho. The BC part of the Interior Plateau is sometimes known as the Canadian Plateau. The environment is characterized by a relatively arid climate and diverse landscape. Though marine resources such as salmon were traditionally significant to the economy, the social and political systems were usually more egalitarian that those of the coast. The characteristic winter dwelling was a semi-subterranean structure commonly known as a pithouse, and although some villages may have had populations of hundreds or more, the overall population density was lower than on the coast. Major ethnic groups customarily regarded as having their traditional territories within the British Columbia portion of the Interior Plateau are the Ktunaxa, Nlaka'pamux, Okanagan, Secwepemc, Stl'atl'imx, and Tsilhqot'in. As the boundaries are not well-defined, the Dakelh are sometimes considered as being within the Interior Plateau and sometimes within the Subarctic. Similarly, residing in southeastern British Columbia, the Ktunaxa are sometimes considered to be one of the Interior Plateau groups and sometimes in the Plains culture area.

The Subarctic culture area includes most of the northern portion of the Canadian provinces. It is bounded by the Arctic culture area on the north, the northern Northwest Coast on the west, and by the Interior Plateau, Plains, and Eastern Woodlands on the south. The environment is characterized by forests, numerous lakes, rivers, muskeg, long cold winters, and relatively short summers. Salmon was an important resource for some groups, but most depended more heavily on other resources, such as moose and caribou. People were more egalitarian, more nomadic, and less populous compared to groups from the Northwest Coast and Interior Plateau. Major ethnic groups within the BC part of the Subarctic are the Dene-thah, Dunne-za, Kaska, Nat'oot'en, Sekani, Tahltan, Wet'suwet'en, and in some interpretations, the northern Dakelh.

Languages

None of the languages of the First Nations within what is now British Columbia had a written form prior to the arrival of Europeans, so the precise number of distinct languages at the time when Europeans first arrived will probably never be known. However, there were probably about fifty. This number is based largely on the number recorded historically and those that have survived to the present despite significant population loss and government policies forbidding the use of First Nations languages, such as in residential schools. Linguists concur that at least eight language families are represented among the languages spoken by First Nations in what is now British Columbia. Languages classified as belonging to the same language family may be as similar as Spanish is to French, and languages classified as belonging to different language families may be as different as English is from Cantonese. Although the specific languages within each family are largely mutually unintelligible, their vocabulary is similar enough to suggest ancestral relationships. That is, the distinct languages in a language family probably evolved from a common language, usually over a few thousand or more years.

Most linguists agree that at least thirty languages native to the First Nations of British Columbia have survived to the present. The problem of reaching consensus on a precise number lies primarily in the difficulty of distinguishing dialects from languages, compounded by the relatively few speakers of many languages and the absence of written forms. Languages are for the most part deemed to be mutually unintelligible, while dialects are deemed to be part of the same language with minor variations in pronunciation, grammar, and vocabulary. Linguists often defer to the language speakers themselves to resolve whether differences are indicative of dialects or wholly distinct languages.

Population

Using First Nations' oral histories, archaeological research, and historical records, many have attempted to estimate the population of First Nations before the influx of Europeans into the region now known as British Columbia. Estimates range from a low of 80,000 to 500,000 or more. Most anthropologists accept population estimates in the 200,000-300,000 range. The highest population densities clearly occurred in the Northwest Coast culture area, followed by the Interior Plateau and Subarctic areas. The Northwest Coast was probably one of the most densely populated areas of North America prior to the arrival of Europeans, and some areas of the coast had higher populations in the past than they do at present.

Settlement Patterns

The Northwest Coast, Interior Plateau, and Subarctic were each distinguished, in part, by settlement patterns. In particular, the three culture areas are characterized by the type of dwelling and the permanence or impermanence of settlements.

Northwest Coast peoples moved throughout their territories for much of the year but returned to large, permanent villages each winter. A winter village consisted of several large cedar plank houses facing the ocean, each accommodating a different kinship group. Cedar plank houses were characteristic of all Northwest Coast groups but they varied widely in style. One of the most obvious distinctions was the external structure, exemplified by the gable roofs and vertical wall planks of the northern nations, in contrast to the shed-type roofs and horizontal planks of the southern nations.

Houses were usually large enough to accommodate several related families, each with its own hearth and living area, as well as a communal area. Families with the lowest rank occupied the part of the house closest to the entrance, which was nearest the beach. The crest of the kinship group occupying the house was often depicted in paintings and carvings on the exterior and sometimes in the interior of the building. Other common features of the houses included wooden shelves, sleeping platforms, and storage boxes.

Haida village of Skidegate, late nineteenth century. The gable roofs, vertical planking, and carved poles are characteristic of winter villages on the north coast. *Courtesy of Royal BC Museum, BC Archives, B-03660*

Winter village populations of the Northwest Coast typically ranged between 200 and 1,000 people. They often broke into smaller family groups during the rest of the year, travelling throughout their traditional territories. People frequently constructed temporary shelters from poles, bark, and vegetation. Some transported the roof and wall planks of a winter dwelling, via canoe, from settlement to settlement, to use in the construction of temporary shelters.

Pithouse. Peoples of the Interior Plateau lived in pithouse villages during winter months. Roofs were typically supported by a log framework and constructed with poles, bark, and a thick layer of earth. Entry was either through a side entrance or via a log ladder through the roof. Pithouse living ceased by the late 1800s, but abandoned pithouses such as the one shown here remained for decades. *Courtesy of Royal BC Museum, BC Archives, G-00754*

In the Interior Plateau, people moved throughout their territories to take advantage of the availability of plants and animals. Like the peoples of the coast, they routinely spent winters in permanent villages, usually in major river valleys. The villages of the Interior Plateau nations were composed of pithouses, a term widely used by anthropologists to describe a semi-subterranean dwelling typically consisting of a circular depression a few metres deep. House diameters ranged from a few to more than twenty metres, but were usually from six to twelve metres. After the depression was excavated, a log framework was erected to support a roof made from poles, bark, and earth. A hole in the centre of the roof served both as a smoke hole and for access. A slanting log with notched steps was used to enter the house through the smoke hole, although some houses also had side entrances.

The houses typically included a central hearth for cooking and warmth, bark-lined storage pits for food, and floors covered with tree boughs. The houses were reused annually. Each house was typically occupied by thirty to forty related people, with an average village population between several dozen and a few hundred people.

During the spring, summer, and autumn, Interior Plateau peoples travelled in smaller family groups and lived in temporary shelters. The shelters were typically constructed with a light pole framework covered with tree boughs, brush, bark, or rush mats, and were not reused.

Although the Ktunaxa live on the periphery of the Interior Plateau, their settlement pattern was more reflective of the Plains culture area. They lived primarily in villages of tipis constructed of pole frameworks covered with hides, and their seasonal round of activities included crossing the Rocky Mountains to hunt buffalo on the Plains.

Unlike the peoples of the Northwest Coast and Interior Plateau, peoples of the Subarctic usually resided in small groups of less than 100 year round, in temporary or portable structures. Their shelters included structures of pole frameworks covered with hides, bark, or brush, sometimes insulated with moss in winter.

Diet

First Nations people throughout all three culture areas incorporated many types of animals into their diet. Seafood, particularly salmon, was an important component for people living near the coast and along the major rivers. Oolichan, sturgeon, herring, trout, and cod were among the many other fish eaten. Invertebrates, such as clams, mussels, cockles, crabs, and urchins, were another common food for coastal peoples. Sea mammals, including seals, porpoises, and whales, were important for some Northwest Coast groups. Terrestrial mammals and birds, such as grouse and ducks,

Salmon Loops (Breakfast Series), 2006. Salmon was a dietary staple of almost all First Nations people in the Northwest Coast and Interior Plateau culture areas, as well as among some Subarctic nations that had direct or trade access. © *Sonny Assu. Image courtesy of the artist and the Equinox Gallery. Photo by Chris Meier*

were a significant part of the diet for most First Nations throughout all culture areas.

Plants were also a significant component of the diets of nations in each culture area. Over 200 species of plants are known to have been used for food, drink, and flavourings. Roots, bulbs, tubers, stems, shoots, buds, leaves, and fruits all provided essential nutrients. Some groups also regularly consumed seeds, nuts, and the inner bark of certain trees.

Recent research indicates that among coastal groups alone, wild plants used for food include about fifty species of berries, such as salal, salmonberries, strawberries, soapberries, huckle-berries, blueberries, and cranberries; twenty-five species of green vegetables, such as horsetail, fireweed, and cow pars-nip; and several species of inner bark, such as alder, cotton-wood, hemlock, fir, and spruce. Several species of marine algae were harvested for food, and about fifty species of plants were used for flavouring, sweeteners, and emergency foods. Among them are parts of sword ferns and tips of hemlock branches used as hunger suppressants, and Sitka spruce for chewing gum.

Technology

First Nations peoples in each culture area employed highly sophisticated technologies for their subsistence activities, such as fishing, hunting, gathering, and cooking, as well for the manufacture of tools, houses, clothing, canoes, jewellery, art, and many other kinds of material culture.

Fish were caught with nets made from natural fibres, spears, baited hooks, and traps. Land mammals and birds were shot with arrows and spears or captured with snares and traps. Sea mammals were hunted with harpoons. Gathering technology included collection baskets made from woven plant materials or bark, and pointed sticks that were sometimes used to dig root crops or shellfish.

Although it would be a stretch to describe their activities as agricultural, or the products of their labour as the creation of domestic plants and animals, there is considerable evidence that First Nations effectively managed their resources to en-hance their productivity long before contact with Europeans. Some First Nations in coastal areas altered beaches in coastal areas by clearing away sticks and rocks to increase the pro-ductivity of shellfish, which were harvested. Some groups transported salmon eggs and smolts to depleted waterways to increase productivity in those systems. Weeding and prun-ing were undertaken to increase productivity of plant foods.

Controlled fires were set to maintain the open habitats preferred by some plants and to enhance the growth of plants used as food by game animals, thus increasing hunting productivity as well. Cooking technology involved roasting food around open fires, boiling, and baking. Since the First Nations had no pottery in which to boil water, they instead used watertight containers made of organic materials. Typically, rocks heated in a fire would be transferred to a container of water, which would then boil with the food in it. Watertight containers used for this purpose included woven baskets, bark baskets, and wooden boxes.

People throughout the world bake in earth ovens, and there are many variations on the idea of using the heat generated by a fire in a pit to cook foods. The technique used by First Nations in what is now British Columbia involved building a fire in a pit, adding meat, fish, shellfish, or edible plants, and then covering them with vegetation and earth. Rocks were often placed around the fire to retain heat. Depending on the food, cooking times varied from less than one hour to three days. Sometimes a vertical stick was placed in the pit to maintain a small hole in the covering, through which water was occasionally poured to create a steaming effect.

Cedar was the most important non-food resource available to people in coastal areas. Not only was cedar the principal component of their houses, it was also used for canoes and for much of their three-dimensional art, such as masks, totem poles, and other wood carvings. The inner bark of cedar was often used to weave baskets, mats, and clothing. Cedar canoes ranged from four to more than twenty metres in length, with a capacity of one to forty people, plus cargo. They were made from a single log hollowed out with hand tools. Fire was sometimes used to assist in hollowing, and boiling water was often used to steam and soften the wood of the canoe, which was then stretched and braced with wood while it cooled. The canoes were often painted with stylistic images of the kinship group that made and used them.

Cedar was not as readily available to groups in the interior, who relied much more on the bark of birch, spruce, and other trees to manufacture their canoes and baskets. Interior groups also tended to use more animal skins in the manufacture of their clothing and dwellings than did coastal groups. Textiles were also manufactured by First Nations, particularly those in coastal regions. Textiles were woven from a variety of plant materials and some animals. Mountain goat hair is known to have been used, and there is speculation that some coastal groups may have bred a small dog specifically for its hair.

Material culture did not include pottery. Most peoples over the past several thousand years with levels of economic and social complexity and sophistication similar to those of the First Nations of British Columbia have made pottery. Its absence in the province may be explained by the extremely efficient basketry technology, which produced containers with many of the benefits of pottery and none of the problems. First Nations people manufactured baskets from materials that were easily available, watertight, and good for storage without being heavy or fragile.

Social Organization
The social organization of First Nations was complex and diverse, particularly in the Northwest Coast culture. Some Interior Plateau and Subarctic nations did exhibit social stratification, but they were generally much more egalitarian than coastal groups. Similarly, control of resources by specific individuals or groups within a community occurred among some interior nations but less commonly than among coastal groups.

Among coastal nations, social organization was based on kinship, social stratification was rigid, and positions of leadership were hereditary. Descent was determined matrilineally among nations of the north coast and bilaterally among nations of the south coast. Material displays of jewellery, clothing, and houses demonstrated high status, as did the giving away of objects. Among some groups, high status was also expressed though a type of cranial shaping. Infants of some high-ranking families had boards tied to their foreheads for extended periods to elongate their skulls.

People of the coast were recognized as belonging to specific houses and clans. A house (the kinship kind) was a group of related extended families living together in one of several large cedar plank houses (the physical kind) making up a winter village, and the leader of the house was the chief, a hereditary position. The house was probably the most important economic, social, and political unit for First Nations in coastal areas. It owned rights to fishing, hunting, and gathering locations, as well as to songs, dances, and stories. The house, under the direction of the chief, generally assigned status, organized subsistence activities, and regulated relations with other groups. Because each house had its own chief, there was no single authority for each village or nation. Although chiefs may have had different status in the village or within the entire nation, decisions affecting the village would have been based on consensus among them.

Clans were groups of related houses from different villages within the territory of the nation. Traditional Nisga'a society, for example, was – and still is – organized into sixty houses, which in turn belong to one of four clans – Raven, Killer Whale, Wolf, and Eagle. Membership in a specific clan was based on a belief that all members descended from a common ancestor, although not all the links were known. Clans were mostly ceremonial units and often depended on symbols – such as Raven, Killer Whale, Wolf, and Eagle for the Nisga'a – to provide members with solidarity and an easy means of identification. It was taboo to marry someone from within one's own clan.

Anthropologists use the categories of band, tribe, chiefdom, and state to describe the social and political organization of peoples throughout the world. Specific types of subsistence – foraging, horticulture, pastoralism, and agriculture – usually correlate with specific types of settlement patterns, economic systems, and other cultural characteristics. Bands, for example, usually depend on hunting and gathering, have fewer than fifty people, are nomadic, and are egalitarian. First Nations of British Columbia, particularly those of the coast, however, do not fit this general pattern. While they depended on wild plants and animals, for example, other characteristics of their culture are more similar to those exhibited by horticultural and agricultural communities. Many anthropologists therefore describe some precolonial First Nations of British Columbia, especially those in coastal areas and in some parts of the Interior Plateau, as complex foragers.

Myths, Spirits, and Shamans

Myths, which are stories about the actions of supernatural beings in the past, are an integral part of all cultures and serve multiple purposes. Myths of the First Nations of British Columbia explain such things as the creation of the world, the features of the landscape, and the occurrence of specific kinds of plants and animals. Myths also explain the origins of people, differences between groups, and values and customs. For many peoples, particularly those in coastal areas, myths are intricately connected with social organization, as status is often tied to the perceived relationship between an individual and a mythological figure. As well, myths are associated with art through their depiction in painting, carving, and performance, and provide education and entertainment.

Myths include characters known as transformers, who could transform themselves and others at will into various animate and inanimate forms. Because they often accomplished their goals through trickery, some transformers are

Siwash Rock. First Nations mythology explains many landforms, often as the work of transformers, who could transform beings into features on the landscape. Siwash Rock in Vancouver is one example. Based on Musqueam and Squamish myth, the inscription on a nearby plaque notes that "this fifty-foot high pinnacle of rock stands as a monument to 'SKALSH the Unselfish,' who was turned into stone by Q'UAS the Transformer." *Photo by Robert Muckle*

also known as tricksters. The best-known tricksters in the mythology of coastal and interior groups are Raven and Coyote respectively. Hundreds of landforms in British Columbia are explained as the work as transformers. One example is Siwash Rock in Vancouver's Stanley Park. According to the myths of the Musqueam and Squamish nations, a man was turned to stone as a permanent reminder of his unselfishness. Two peaks in the Coast Mountain Range, popularly known as The Lions for their appearance of lions at rest, are described by some First Nations as The Sisters, referring to the myth that the peaks are two daughters of an important chief who convinced their father to seek peace rather than war, and were subsequently immortalized in the mountains.

First Nations people believed in the existence of many types of spirits. As well as recognizing a human spirit, for example, they believed that animals, plants, and other natural

Sasquatch

Stories of large, hairy, human- or ape-like animals inhabiting the forested regions of British Columbia are legion. For about the last hundred years these animals have been widely known as sasquatch, which is an anglicized version of the Halkomelem word for the creature. Halkomelem is the language of the Fraser Valley First Nations, who write the word as "sasq'ets" or something similar. Most First Nations languages have a specific word for some kind of human- or ape-like being (not necessarily always large). Among some other First Nations of the province, they are known as wild men, wild women, or wild people. More widely, across North America they are also known as bigfoot.

Commonly reported characteristics of sasquatch include being bipedal (habitually walking upright), almost always being solitary, vocalizing through screams, and avoiding human contact.

Some First Nations consider sasquatch spiritual, but mostly they are simply included as part of narratives or storytelling. They are often described as being very strong and fast, but they do not have supernatural powers. Generally, among First Nations, sasquatch are creatures to be avoided. Often phenomena such as fallen trees and boulders falling down slopes are considered to be the work of sasquatch.

phenomena such as rivers, lakes, and mountains had spirits. This belief system, known as animism, is found in nations throughout the world. Guardian spirits were also recognized by many First Nations. They were believed to bestow power during vision quests. Vision quests were usually carried out in solitude by most males, and some females, after puberty. During the quest, a guardian spirit would manifest itself to the individual and bestow powers that would protect that person and enhance his or her actions.

Shamanism was another important element of First Nations cultures. A shaman was a person, usually a man, with a unique ability to deal with supernatural beings. Shamans could obtain their expertise through birth, training, or a special encounter. They had a variety of responsibilities, including interpreting events, ensuring successful foraging or warring expeditions, and curing people when the cause of illness was thought to be spiritual. A common diagnosis by a shaman was soul loss – when a person's soul had left the body. As a cure, a shaman could visit the spirit world to retrieve the soul.

Health and Healing

It is generally thought that First Nations people of British Columbia were well nourished and relatively free from high-mortality epidemic diseases before the arrival of Europeans. Important factors in maintaining good health included the relatively small size of their settlements, a hygienic lifestyle, a varied diet, and knowledge of natural medicines.

First Nations recognized two distinct types of ailments: spiritual and physical. Spiritual ailments were usually treated by shamans. Physical ailments could be treated by any knowledgeable member of the community. They were proficient at mending broken or dislocated limbs using splints and treating infected teeth and gums through cauterization. Treatment of other physical ailments tended to depend on knowledge of the healing properties of plants. People in most nations used at least a few dozen different plants as medicines. Sweat lodges were an important element of spiritual and physical healing. Accommodating from one to several people, most sweat lodges were rounded structures made with a pole framework overlaid with earth, mats, or brush. Much as in a modern-day sauna or steam bath, water was poured over hot rocks to create high humidity and heat inside the structure. In addition to their hygienic value, sweat baths were commonly thought to enhance the effectiveness of plant medicines and to provide spiritual cleansing. Sweat baths were also part of ritual preparations for hunting, fishing, and warring expeditions.

Art

Art was an important component of all First Nations cultures. Visual arts such as carving, sculpture, and paintings, and performing arts such as dance, music, and storytelling, were all practised.

First Nations people in all culture areas routinely decorated baskets and other utilitarian objects. Art was most pervasive among coastal groups, however, where clothing, jewellery, storage boxes, and tools regularly featured designs. Coastal peoples were also distinguished by extensive wood sculpture, including carved and painted masks, and totem, house, and mortuary poles.

The designs of Subarctic and Interior Plateau peoples were conventionally simple. Designs on baskets, for example, were often geometric. They had aesthetic value and may have indicated ownership. Paintings and sculptures were relatively rare.

Designs of Northwest Coast peoples, by contrast, were often complex and highly symbolic. Paintings and low-relief sculptures, in particular, often became abstract. The use of broad black form lines, ovoids, U- and S-forms, splitting, symmetry, space-filling, and stylized motifs to depict creatures has come to characterize the Northwest Coast art style. Splitting involves creating an image that is mirrored along an axis. Space-filling involves covering the entire surface of a painting or sculpture, leaving no or little space between figures or images. Although Northwest Coast art had aesthetic value, its primary function is thought to have been symbolic. Paintings and sculpture usually reflected kinship. Totem poles, house poles, and mortuary poles depicted lines of descent. Paintings, carvings, tattoos, and clothing often depicted clan affiliation.

The function of pictographs (paintings on rock) and petroglyphs (carvings on rock) throughout the culture areas is often unclear. They are frequently found in places with difficult access and have simple designs. Pictographs are often painted over one another. Some were probably created to record events and identify territory. Much of the art is thought to be the work of shamans attempting to influence supernatural beings or of individuals on vision quests. The simplicity of the designs and the practice of superimposing one image over another suggest that at many rock art locations, the process was more important than the product.

The performing arts of First Nations included storytelling, dance, and music, frequently as part of social and spiritual events. Myths, legends, and tales were commonly told at feasts and other ceremonies. Although dance and music were sometimes separate performances, they could accompany storytelling. Dancers often wore costumes with masks, and instruments included drums made from wood and hide, and rattles made from wood, pebbles, and deer or goat hooves. Like many other aspects of culture, some stories, dances, and music were subject to ownership by individuals or kinship groups.

The Potlatch and Other Important Ceremonies
The potlatch ceremony usually took place in winter and could last a few weeks or more. At a potlatch, the host group would

announce that an event of social and political significance had occurred or was about to occur. As well as an announcement, the ceremony involved recitation of oral history, feasting, dancing, singing, and the distribution of gifts to guests. Guests typically included members from other villages from within the same ethnic group. Although some interior nations have held potlatches in the past few hundred years, they are associated most closely with coastal groups.

The manifest function of a potlatch was usually to validate a socially and politically meaningful event, such as a person's formal assumption of the role of chief. The recitation of oral history, supported by dancing and singing, led to the announcement. The guests acted as witnesses, and their acceptance of gifts indicated acceptance of the announcement. Latent functions of the potlatch included the redistribution of wealth through gift giving, the maintenance of alliances, and the opportunity to put on public record (for the host and guest groups) all important changes in a group, such as births, marriages, deaths, and transfer of rights. Events at potlatches also affirmed an individual's identity and status through the way he or she was treated, provided an opportunity to forge new relationships between individuals and groups, and educated and entertained people.

Potlatches were not the only major ceremonies that gathered people from various communities. Many First Nations regularly had ceremonies with large attendance from multiple villages but without the gift-giving feature of the potlatch. Like the potlatch, the ceremonies helped create and maintain economic, social, and political relationships.

Ceremonialism was also closely linked with both subsistence and spiritualism. It was not uncommon, for example, for First Nations people to undertake ritualistic dancing, singing, and sweat bathing prior to a foraging expedition. A first salmon ceremony, in which the first salmon taken in the season was ritually treated and placed back in the water, was common among Northwest Coast and Interior Plateau nations.

Trade, Slavery, and Warfare

Trade between villages and between nations was common. Many kinds of preserved foods were exchanged. Interior groups without direct access to coastal resources often traded for dried fish, exchanging hides and furs. Oolichan, caught mostly by nations of the central coast, was particularly prized; some of the well-known trading routes in the province became known as "grease trails" in reference to the oil rendered from the fish. Manufactured items such as baskets and cedar canoes were often exchanged, as were raw materials such as shell and obsidian.

Slavery was common among First Nations, particularly among coastal nations and to a lesser extent in the Interior Plateau. Most slaves were captives of war or the children of captives, and it is reported that they constituted up to 30 percent of the population of some villages. Among some nations, a woman and her children lost their status as slaves if she married one of the local men. Slaves were often traded and sometimes ransomed. They not only were valued for their labour but also provided their owners with a means of exhibiting social rank. Some individuals reportedly had as many as fifty slaves. Slaves had a very low status, of course, and were sometimes distinguished by markers such as a particular haircut. While many slaves came from ethnic groups different from their captors, it was not uncommon for slaves to be taken captive by members of the same ethnic group residing in a different village.

Violent conflict was pervasive among some coastal groups. Fighting could occur in many contexts, and conflicts between different kinship groups within the same nation were not uncommon. Organized war expeditions occurred throughout the coastal regions, with the capture of slaves or revenge the primary motivations. Typically, a group attacked at dawn, using the element of surprise. Men were often killed, and women and children taken captive. War parties ranged from a few to hundreds of warriors. Protective clothing and shields were sometimes used, and some villages were fortified.

Recommended Readings and Resources

The Handbook of North American Indians is an excellent source for information on traditional lifeways of many different nations in what is now British Columbia. The relevant specific volumes are *Subarctic*, edited by June Helm (Washington, DC: Smithsonian Institution, 1981), *Northwest Coast*, edited by Wayne Suttles (Washington, DC: Smithsonian Institution, 1990), and *Plateau*, edited by Deward Walker (Washington, DC: Smithsonian Institution, 1998). Ralph Maud's *A Guide to B.C. Indian Myth and Legend* (Vancouver: Talonbooks, 1982) includes information on many of the anthropologists working in British Columbia in the late 1800s and early 1900s, and the ethnographies they produced. Ethnology on the Northwest Coast is the focus of *Coming to Shore: Northwest Coast Ethnology, Traditions, and Visions*, edited by Marie Mauze, Michael E. Harkin, and Sergei Kan (Lincoln: University of Nebraska Press, 2004). An overview of how First Nations managed food resources in precolonial times is provided in *Keeping It Living: Traditions of Plant Use and Cultivation on the Northwest Coast of North America*, edited by Douglas Deur and Nancy Turner (Vancouver: UBC Press, 2005).

Nancy Turner has written multiple books on the use of plants by First Nations, including *Plant Technology of First Peoples in British Columbia* (Vancouver: UBC Press, 1998), *Food Plants of Interior First Peoples* (Vancouver: UBC Press, 1997), and *Food Plants of Coastal First Peoples* (Vancouver: UBC Press, 1995).

lacer Mining
ompson River

Part 5

From the Late 1700s through the Twentieth Century

Beginning with the fur trade in the late eighteenth century, the population, economy, technology, social organization, and many other aspects of First Nations cultures have changed significantly. In addition to governments, the major agents of change have been fur traders, gold seekers, settlers, and religious orders. This part outlines the impact of these agents. This part also provides an overview of assertions of Aboriginal rights, negotiations in the late 1900s, and the changing nature of anthropology in the latter part of the twentieth century.

Population Loss

From an estimated population of at least 200,000 in the mid-1700s, the number of First Nations people in what is now British Columbia declined to about 100,000 by 1835. By 1885 the population had dropped to 28,000, and by 1929 the population was down to 23,000. This was most likely the lowest population number for several thousand years, and may represent a reduction of more than 90 percent. Even using a very conservative estimate of 100,000 for the eighteenth-century population, the overall loss was at least 75 percent. Numbers began to increase after 1929.

The major cause of this massive population decline was diseases carried by Europeans to North America and for which First Nations people had no natural immunity. They also had little access to vaccinations. Deadly diseases included smallpox, tuberculosis, scarlet fever, influenza, and measles. Smallpox was the most devastating of all the diseases, and major epidemics occurred in British Columbia in the late 1700s, the late 1830s, and the early 1860s.

Europeans also introduced First Nations people to alcohol and firearms, both of which contributed to population loss. In some cases alcohol led to death from accidents, and in other cases to social problems and infertility, with consequently fewer births. Although firearms almost certainly increased rates of mortality from conflict, including conflicts between First Nations, the impact on population was minor compared to that of smallpox and other diseases.

No nation was spared the devastation of significant population loss, which affected every aspect of First Nations cultures. As leaders, healers, weavers, carvers, keepers of oral history, and other specialists died, often no one could take their place. Sometimes cultural knowledge was lost forever. It is likely, for example, that at least several languages were lost as well as information about the medicinal value of some plants. Dwindling numbers also led to changes in subsistence and settlement patterns. Some groups could no longer maintain the traditional round of hunting, fishing, and gathering plants. Social and political structures were often thrown into disarray as population loss blurred the once clear relationships between individuals and between groups.

The Impact of the Fur Trade

The first encounters between First Nations and people of European descent occurred in the 1770s. A Spanish ship sailed up and down the Pacific coast in 1774, making contact with at least a few First Nations. Shortly after, British and American vessels began an intense period of trading with coastal nations. By the early nineteenth century the land-based fur trade was established with interior nations.

First Nations were willing participants in the fur trade, and nations, villages, and leaders appear to have competed for access to European and American traders. Not all First Nations got along with the traders, however, and although rare, violent confrontation did occur, sometimes resulting in death on both sides.

Interaction with First Nations was a business relationship for the fur traders. Their primary objective was to obtain furs for the least possible cost, and there is no reliable evidence that they had any deliberate plan to bring epidemics to the people or to change their cultures. Inadvertently, however, the fur trade did result in significant changes in traditional lifeways – in material culture, subsistence, and settlement patterns. Many new items of trade were introduced to First Nations, such as metal tools and wool blankets. Metal carving tools enhanced woodworking, and metal pots and kettles made cooking easier. Subsistence and other economic activities were altered by some individuals and groups to obtain more fur for trade. More hunting and trapping of fur-bearing animals, such as otters, occurred at the expense of other activities. By acting as brokers or intermediaries in the fur trade, some groups became less nomadic, and many First Nations started to settle near the trading posts.

The fur trade also altered relationships between nations and between individuals. Some nations developed more power than formerly because their strategic location or influence with the traders enabled them to control trade. Leaders of some nations were able to strengthen their positions and accumulate more wealth by serving as primary negotiators.

Traditional lifeways also changed as new markets were created for arts and crafts. Shortly after trade began in the late eighteenth century, traders began to seek arts and crafts as well as furs, and some individuals responded by specializing in the creation of arts and crafts, including wood carvings, for trade.

The Impact of the Gold Rushes

Some gold seekers from the United States arrived on the north coast and southern interior regions of the province before the late 1850s, but they were forcibly driven away by First Nations. The sheer number of gold seekers eventually became too great for First Nations to control, however, and their impact was soon felt.

Major gold rushes in 1858 along the Fraser and Thompson Rivers, in the 1860s in the Cariboo, and in the 1870s in the north brought about 30,000 gold seekers, mostly of European descent, into the province. They destroyed fish habitats in river systems, contributed to changes in First Nations economic activities, and altered relationships between First Nations and people of European descent. Unlike fur traders, who depended on First Nations for the supply of furs, most gold seekers had no need or wish to accommodate First Nations. They were not interested in creating or maintaining long-term relationships with First Nations people. As well, many of the gold seekers came directly from the gold rushes of California, where there was a history of poor relations and violence against Native American peoples. Many gold seekers brought an attitude of superiority into British Columbia, and there are numerous reports of conflicts between them and First Nations.

The gold seekers also affected the economic organizations of First Nations. First Nations people understood the value of gold, and many became gold seekers themselves. Others gave up their traditional subsistence activities in order to work for wages providing services to the gold seekers. Many First Nations people traditionally dependent on salmon had to alter their diet because fewer fish were available to them. Many of the salmon were being taken by and for gold seekers before First Nations people had a chance to catch them. In other cases, spawning areas were destroyed by mining activities.

The Impact of Non-Indigenous Settlement

Although there were some earlier attempts at settlement, settlers did not arrive in British Columbia in significant numbers until 1858. Some came directly from Britain and elsewhere to establish homesteads; others simply decided to stay after the gold rushes.

Possibly because of the common belief that the First Nations people were doomed to extinction anyway, the settlers did not have a deliberate plan to alter First Nations lifeways.

Gold miners along the Thompson River. Many First Nations people, such as those depicted here, joined the gold rushes of the mid- and late 1880s. *Courtesy of Royal BC Museum, BC Archives, D-06815*

First Nations people were viewed primarily as a hindrance, and major conflicts between First Nations and settlers occurred over land. Like the gold seekers, the settlers came with an attitude of superiority.

With the support of colonial governments, settlers were able to take control of many of the traditional territories of First Nations. Consequently, many First Nations people were unable to carry out their traditional subsistence activities. In order to support themselves and their families, they had to leave their villages to look for work in the larger towns created by colonial settlement. This migration often led to the breakdown of traditional social relations and increased dependence of First Nations people on settlers.

Missionaries and Residential Schools

Although the history of missionaries in British Columbia extends back into the late eighteenth century, their impact on

First Nations was negligible until the late nineteenth century. A First Nations perspective on the introduction of Christianity, particularly the impact of missionary Alfred Hall, is described by Gloria Cranmer Webster in "From Colonization to Repatriation":

> The introduction of Christianity must have been a confusing time for our people. At the same time [as] missionaries like Hall were preaching, "Thou shalt not steal," settlers were helping themselves to large tracts of land ... While Hall was telling the people that, "It is better to give than to receive," he was also telling them that lavish gift-giving at potlatches was sinful and heathenish. With all the mixed messages the missionaries were giving the local people, it is no wonder that there were few converts. People had difficulty making sense of it all. (p. 29)

However, by the early twentieth century many First Nations people had been converted to Christianity. As anthropologist Wilson Duff notes in *The Indian History of British Columbia*, "By 1904, 90 per cent of the Indians of the Province were nominally Christian" (p. 87). One explanation is that significant population loss and severe disruptions to traditional lifeways during the nineteenth century prompted many First Nations people to follow missionary teachings. During the initial fur trade period, conditions for most First Nations people had likely stayed more or less the same or improved. As the impact of gold seekers and settlers became felt, however, living conditions deteriorated and many First Nations people may have become disillusioned. They may have begun to accept Christianity to explain or cope with the severe population loss and the economic, social, and political domination they were experiencing.

Unlike the fur traders, gold seekers, and settlers, missionaries had deliberate plans to change the traditional lifeways

Metlakatla, 1880s. This community was established among the Tsimshian in the 1860s by a missionary, William Duncan, with a view to assimilating First Nations people into Euro-Canadian society. *Courtesy of Royal BC Museum, BC Archives, G-04699*

of First Nations. Their intent was to alter First Nations cultures completely, encouraging agrarian settlement and abandonment of traditional ceremonies and beliefs.

One well-known missionary, William Duncan, went so far as to set up a new Tsimshian community at Metlakatla in the 1860s. For its nearly 1,000 residents he established a set of rules forbidding such traditional cultural elements as shamanism and potlatching and making mandatory such practices as religious instruction and payment of taxes. In his attempt to get First Nations people away from what he considered bad influences and to assimilate them into Euro-Canadian society, Duncan was doing what later church workers and governments would attempt, beginning in the 1880s, through the residential school system.

The residential school system was based on the notions that assimilation was best for First Nations people and that the best method of assimilation was to remove children from their homes and teach them the ways of Euro-Canadian society in schools where they also lived. The Canadian government made and enforced the rules, such as mandatory attendance, and provided most of the funding, while the Roman Catholic, Anglican, Methodist, Baptist, Presbyterian, and United Churches operated the schools. The policy of most residential schools was first to break all the children's cultural ties to language, family, and traditional lifeways, and then to re-educate them in Christian and Euro-Canadian ways. Children were commonly given new names, physically abused for speaking their languages, and taught that the ways of their parents were evil.

The residential school system had a severe impact on First Nations people and their cultures. Reports of physical, sexual, and emotional abuse of First Nations children attending residential schools began in the late nineteenth century and have continued into the twenty-first century. The schools also contributed to the loss of many traditional lifeways, such as languages and knowledge about healing, parenting, and social relations. Extended periods of school residence frequently led to family breakdown. Children were often unable to communicate with their parents and had little in common with them.

First Nations children attending residential schools usually received a poorer education than other children in the province. Even in the mid-twentieth century, government spending on First Nations children in residential schools was less than 25 percent of that for non-First Nations children. Also, First Nations children in residential schools received less education in academic subjects because many residential schools focused on instruction in farming and trades.

The impact of residential schools has long been a source of controversy. Many First Nations people did not want to be part of the system. However, some First Nations people saw attendance at the schools as a useful means of learning how to coexist with Euro-Canadians. As well, some First Nations converts to Christianity saw the residential schools as an effective way of spreading the faith.

As a mechanism for assimilating First Nations people into Euro-Canadian society, the residential school system is widely acknowledged to have failed, and some of the Churches as well as the federal government have recently made public apologies (see Appendix 4). As long ago as 1947 Diamond Jenness, a prominent anthropologist, declared that the residential schools were a failure and recommended their abolition, but the last residential school in British Columbia did not close until 1984.

First Nations and Wage Labour

As populations dwindled and their resources and lands were appropriated by settlers in the late nineteenth century, it became increasingly difficult, and in many cases impossible, for First Nations to maintain their traditional economic systems. Many First Nations people consequently turned to the new major industries of commercial fishing, logging, farming, ranching, mining, and transportation. Some First Nations people were able to operate their own businesses, but many obstacles prevented success. Laws prevented them from selling fish, denied them water licences for irrigation, and limited the amount of good land they could acquire for farming. While a settler simply had to improve up to 320 acres of land to become its owner, this process, known as pre-emption, was not available to First Nations people.

With few or no other options, many First Nations people entered the new economies as part of the labour force. Some anthropologists and historians suggest this fundamentally changed the relationship between First Nations people and others. Instead of being recognized as trading partners, First Nations people came to be viewed by many as simply part of a pool of labourers.

Chinook Trade Language

Communication within the Pacific Northwest for much of the last few hundred years was facilitated by the use of what is commonly called the Chinook trade language. Since there is some debate about whether it should truly be classified as a language, some prefer to call it Chinook Jargon.

This language, or jargon, was initially based on the vocabulary of the Chinook peoples of the Lower Columbia River region of Oregon, but also included words from other languages in the Pacific Northwest. Some believe the Chinook Jargon emerged only with the arrival of Europeans, but it probably developed much earlier, perhaps thousands of years earlier, for communication between various First Nations groups.

Chinook Jargon became very widely used in interactions between First Nations people and people of European descent as well as between First Nations people unfamiliar with each other's languages, who increasingly found themselves in each other's company as a result of colonialization. English, and to a lesser extent, French, words found their way into the vocabulary. Traders, settlers, missionaries, and government officials were all likely to have been familiar with the Chinook trade language.

Multiple dictionaries were produced in the late 1800s and early 1900s, and one BC newspaper was even written in the Chinook Jargon. English eventually took over as the dominant language, but Chinook Jargon remained in some use, particularly in remote places like coastal canneries, until the mid-1900s. Following are some examples:

Chinook	English
boston	American
chuck	water
cultus	worthless
dolla	dollar, or money
hyack	fast
kikweelie	below or beneath
klahanie	outdoors
muckamuck	eat, drink
potlatch	to give
saltchuck	ocean
siwash	Native
skookum	strong
tillicum	friend or relative

Government Relations with First Nations

One of the most important documents governing relations between First Nations and the non-Indigenous Canadian governments is the Royal Proclamation issued by King George III in 1763 (Appendix 5). The proclamation was issued to maintain peace and a sense of order between British subjects and Indigenous peoples in North America. It asserted that Indigenous peoples had existing rights and established the system of surrendering those rights by treaty. Since no European had yet been to the area now known as British Columbia when the proclamation was made, some view it as having little value in regard to protecting the rights of First Nations in the province. Others see it as a guarantee of the rights of all Indigenous peoples on the continent, including those in British Columbia.

Before the mid-1800s, there was relatively little conflict over First Nations rights in what is now British Columbia, probably because the colonial governments vested responsibility for relations with First Nations with traders. The traders were focused on maintaining exchange networks and had little interest in broader issues of First Nations rights, including the ramifications of the Royal Proclamation and treaties.

Colonial government policies, including the Royal Proclamation, began to have a significant impact on First Nations in the mid-1800s with the official establishment of British colonies in what is now British Columbia. Vancouver Island was made a colony in 1849, and most of what is now mainland British Columbia was made a colony in 1858.

One of the most influential people of the late nineteenth century in relations between First Nations and colonial governments was James Douglas. Douglas was a long-time Hudson's Bay Company employee with an extensive history of work in the region. While with the Hudson's Bay Company Douglas had worked with First Nations on Vancouver

Island and the mainland. Later, as governor of Vancouver Island from 1851 to 1858 and of the colony of British Columbia from 1858 until his retirement in 1864, he was responsible for government relations with First Nations. Following the spirit of the Royal Proclamation, Douglas made fourteen treaties with First Nations on Vancouver Island between 1851 and 1854, now widely known as the Douglas treaties. These treaties allowed the nations continuing rights to hunt and fish in their traditional territories. Neither the British government nor the provincial assembly would provide the necessary funds for further treaties after 1854, but Douglas did continue to confer with First Nations and to lay out reserves.

Douglas is often portrayed as being sympathetic to First Nations concerns. He recognized Aboriginal rights, consulted First Nations when laying out reserves, and sought peacekeepers with knowledge of First Nations to maintain order and resolve conflicts between First Nations and non-First Nations people, especially the gold seekers and settlers moving into the colonies. Douglas also advised First Nations to use British law to seek retribution or compensation for perceived wrongs.

Following Douglas's retirement in 1864, the person responsible for government relations with First Nations was Joseph Trutch. As chief commissioner for lands and works and later as lieutenant governor, Trutch was active in creating policy until his retirement in 1880. He viewed First Nations as a hindrance to the development of British Columbia. He often spoke of First Nations in a derogatory manner, reduced the size of their reserves, and denied all forms of Aboriginal rights. In no sense whatsoever did Trutch follow the spirit of the Royal Proclamation.

The allocation of reserves, which began in the mid-1800s, involved colonial, provincial, and federal governments. In the early 1860s Governor James Douglas established the reserve system in British Columbia. His policy is unclear, but indications are that he viewed ten acres per family as a minimum allocation. When Trutch assumed responsibility for First Nations he arbitrarily decreased the size of some reserves established by Douglas and set ten acres per family as a maximum for new reserves. For comparison, the standard formulas used in Ontario and the Prairie provinces were 80 and 640 acres per family respectively. Although there is some doubt whether the federal government knew of the BC government policies and practices regarding First Nations, including the ten-acre maximum, the terms of union entrenched the formula when British Columbia joined Canada in 1871. In 1924 the federal government passed a bill that made decreasing the size of reserves without the consent of First Nations legal.

When British Columbia joined Canada, the primary responsibility for government relations with First Nations was transferred to the federal government. Of the many federal government acts, policies, accords, and commissions affecting the First Nations of British Columbia, several stand out: the Indian Act, the Statement of the Government of Canada on Indian Policy, the Canadian Constitution, and the Royal Commission on Aboriginal Peoples.

First passed in 1876 and having undergone several revisions since, the Indian Act governs relations between First Nations and the Canadian government. Many people see the act as paternalistic and detrimental to First Nations in Canada. Governing such things as the acquisition of status, election of chiefs and councils, use of reserves, management of money, and education, the Indian Act is viewed by some as structuring inequality and poverty. It is also often seen as a mechanism to destroy First Nations cultures and to restrict protests and litigation. For example, previous versions of the Indian Act outlawed potlatches and the hiring of lawyers to pursue land claims.

THE HAPPIEST FUTURE
★
FOR THE
INDIAN RACE IS
★
ABSORPTION
★
INTO THE GENERAL POPULATION
★
THIS IS THE POLICY OF OUR GOVERNMENT

★ DUNCAN CAMPBELL SCOTT ★

Happiest Future #6, 2012.
The policy and practice of the federal government toward First Nations people in British Columbia was assimilation. In this artwork, Sonny Assu takes the words of Duncan Campbell Scott, head of the Department of Indian and Northern Affairs (1913-32) and puts them in poster form. © *Sonny Assu. Image courtesy of Sonny Assu and the Equinox Gallery*

Prohibitions against the potlatch were first introduced in the 1880s and strengthened in later versions of the act. Section 140 of the 1927 version of the Indian Act states:

Every Indian or other person who engages in, or assists in celebrating or encourages either directly or indirectly another to celebrate any Indian festival, dance or other ceremony of which the giving away or paying or giving back of money, goods or articles of any sort forms a part, or is a feature, whether such gift of money, goods or articles takes place before, at, or after the celebration of the same … is guilty of an offence and is liable on summary conviction to imprisonment for a term not exceeding six months and not less than two months.

Live from the 'Latch, 2012. Prohibitions against potlatching were introduced in the 1880s and made stronger in later versions of the Indian Act. Potlatching remained illegal until 1951. © *Sonny Assu. Artwork by Sonny Assu; image courtesy of the artist*

Many people went to prison for participating in potlatches, and many of the masks and other objects present at potlatches were confiscated. Some confiscated items were sent to museums while others were either kept or sold by government workers. Many Euro-Canadians found the potlatch objectionable, presumably because they did not understand it. Instead of appreciating the economic, social, and political significance of the event, they interpreted attendance and participation as a lengthy leisure activity for individuals who should have been working. The idea of giving material objects away to gain status was foreign to Euro-Canadians. As well, its status as a First Nations custom contravened the Canadian government policy of assimilation. Potlatching remained illegal until 1951.

In response to increasing protests from First Nations over abuses of their rights, the federal government legislated against hiring lawyers to pursue land claims. Section 141 of the 1927 version of the Indian Act states:

> Every person who, without the consent of the Superintendent General expressed in writing, receives, obtains, solicits, or requests from any Indian any payment or contribution or promise of any payment or contribution for the purpose of raising a fund or providing money for the prosecution of any claim which the tribe or band of Indians to which such Indian belongs, or of which he is a member, has or is represented to have for the recovery of any claim or money for the benefit of the said tribe or band, shall be guilty of an offence and liable upon summary conviction for each such offence to a penalty not exceeding two hundred dollars and not less than fifty dollars or to imprisonment for any term not exceeding two months.

Notwithstanding the potentially detrimental effects of the Indian Act on First Nations people, many also see positive consequences. It provides special status to First Nations people, it offers some protection of Aboriginal rights, such as the maintenance of reserves, and it provides for such benefits as medical care and education.

In 1969 the federal government released a document entitled "Statement of the Government of Canada on Indian Policy," which became widely known as the White Paper. It proposed the complete assimilation of First Nations into Canadian culture by the abolition of Indian status, the Indian Act, and the Department of Indian Affairs. Reaction to the White Paper by First Nations in British Columbia and elsewhere in Canada was negative, and the proposal was subsequently withdrawn. While they had not been pleased with the paternalistic nature of the federal government policies concerning their affairs, First Nations leaders viewed the proposal as an elimination of their legislative protection and a denial of Aboriginal rights. Leaders were also angry that they had not been consulted by the federal government about the proposed changes in policy, as had been promised. Because the White Paper proposed assimilation, in which there would be no special status or rights, it is somewhat ironic that it provided a focus of opposition that bonded many First Nations. For example, the Union of British Columbia Indian Chiefs, a group that remains politically active, was created in response to the White Paper.

Another federal government act with important consequences for First Nations was the patriation and revision of the Canadian Constitution in 1985. Section 35 of the Constitution states:

(1) The existing aboriginal and treaty rights of the aboriginal peoples of Canada are hereby recognized and affirmed.

(2) In this Act, "aboriginal peoples of Canada" includes the Indian, Inuit and Métis peoples of Canada.

(3) For greater certainty, in subsection (1) "treaty rights" includes rights that now exist by way of land claims agreement or may be so acquired.

(4) Notwithstanding any other provision of this Act, the aboriginal and treaty rights referred to in subsection (1) are guaranteed equally to male and female persons.

Subsections (1) and (2) were part of the original Constitution of 1982. Subsections (3) and (4) were added by the Constitution Amendment Proclamation, 1983. Recognition of Aboriginal rights in the Constitution has prompted various court cases and treaty negotiations. Although it affirms the existence of Aboriginal rights, definition of those rights has been left to the courts.

Another part of the Constitution with significant implications for First Nations is the Canadian Charter of Rights and Freedoms. Section 25 of the Charter states:

> The guarantee in this Charter of certain rights and freedoms shall not be construed so as to abrogate or derogate from any aboriginal, treaty or other rights or freedoms that pertain to the aboriginal peoples of Canada including
>
> (a) any rights or freedoms that have been recognized by the Royal Proclamation of October 7, 1763; and
> (b) any rights or freedoms that now exist by way of land claims settlement or may be so acquired.

The Charter also guarantees equality between the sexes, which led the federal government in 1985 to pass Bill C-31, An Act to Amend the Indian Act, eliminating sexual discrimination in the act. Prior to that a woman and her children faced automatic loss of Indian status if she married an non-Indian man. Bill C-31 is also significant because it provided First Nations with the option of controlling their own membership – determining who could be a member of their nation – and allowed for the restoration of status to those who had either voluntarily relinquished it or lost it through previous legislation.

Although the Meech Lake Accord was blocked and the Charlottetown Accord was defeated in a national referendum, both had important implications for First Nations in British Columbia and elsewhere in Canada. Discussion among politicians, Aboriginal leaders, and the public raised the profile of First Nations peoples, organizations, and issues.

Formulated in 1987 between the prime minister and provincial premiers, the Meech Lake Accord described Quebec as a "distinct society" but failed to recognize the concerns of Aboriginal people in Canada. Aboriginal leaders articulated their concerns to the Canadian public and helped block passage of the accord in 1990, to the pleasure of many First Nations people and other Canadians opposed to the accord for a variety of reasons.

At least partly due to the issues raised about the Meech Lake Accord, the federal government invited Aboriginal leaders to participate in the development of the Charlottetown Accord. As a result, First Nations issues, including the recognition of an inherent right to self-government, were addressed in the document. Although the Charlottetown Accord was defeated in a 1992 referendum, the role of Aboriginal people in the process was significant. It was the first time that they had been treated as equals in such important discussions about the relations between First Nations and governments and the future of Canada.

In 1991, the federal government established a royal commission, made up of both Aboriginal and non-Aboriginal people, to investigate issues concerning Aboriginal peoples. After five years of study, at an estimated cost of $58 million, the commission released its five-volume report in 1996. Its central conclusion was that "the main policy direction, pursued for more than 150 years, first by colonial then by Canadian governments, has been wrong." Major recommendations included the creation of an Aboriginal parliament and increased spending on Aboriginal programs for the next fifteen to twenty years, presumably improving economic and social conditions to the extent that the short-term influx of money would lead to long-term financial savings for all Canadians.

In 1998 the federal government made its first official response to the report of the royal commission, stating, "The government of Canada today formally expresses to all Aboriginal people in Canada our profound regret for past actions of the federal government which have contributed to these difficult pages in the history of our relationships together." As well as the expression of regret, the government created a $350-million healing fund and promised $250 million, spread out over four years, in addition to the existing funding for Aboriginal peoples. The commission had recommended an increase in spending of $1.5 billion to $2 billion per year over fifteen to twenty years.

While the federal government received some credit for following through with the healing fund, to the dismay of many it failed to respond to the vast majority of commission recommendations, including those on constitutional matters such as an Aboriginal parliament, the twenty-year agenda for change, and the substantial increases in spending. One recommendation that has been implemented is the establishment of National Aboriginal Day. Since 1996 the day has been celebrated on 21 June and is marked in communities across the country with displays and performances by Aboriginals in public venues.

Assertions of Aboriginal Rights
First Nations in British Columbia have a long history of asserting their rights by protests, petitions, confrontations, litigation, and negotiation. Throughout the late nineteenth and early twentieth centuries, First Nations across the province held large assemblies protesting denial of Aboriginal rights, lack of government willingness to negotiate treaties, and the small size of reserves. These assemblies sometimes led to formal petitions to provincial, federal, and British governments, and representatives of First Nations travelled to Victoria, Ottawa, and England to seek redress. The routine response of governments was inaction.

Confrontation has long been used to assert Aboriginal rights in the province. There are many accounts of First Nations resisting the actions of Euro-Canadians by making threats, confiscating survey equipment, and resorting to violence. One of the best-known examples is the "Chilcotin wars," in which more than a dozen road builders and settlers were killed by members of the Tsilhqot'in nation attempting to protect their land and lifeways in 1864. Confrontation in the form of blockades became common in the 1980s and 1990s. Blocking roads and railways has often been a means of pressuring governments and corporations to negotiate outstanding claims and issues, often with success and rarely escalating into violence.

The most violent confrontation in recent decades occurred at Gustafsen Lake, near 100 Mile House in the Cariboo. The right to occupy a sacred site was at the heart of a conflict between a few dozen First Nations people and their supporters and approximately 400 RCMP officers and military personnel. Although there were injuries, the standoff ended without anyone being killed. Charges against fourteen First Nations people and four of their non-First Nations supporters ranged from attempted murder to criminal mischief and possession of weapons. A 1997 jury verdict resulted in four people being convicted of possessing weapons and of mischief endangering life, eleven people being convicted of wilful mischief, and three people being acquitted.

Many First Nations have chosen to assert their rights through the courts. Among the most significant cases are *Calder* (1973), *Sparrow* (1990), and *Delgamuukw* (1997).

In the *Calder* case, the Nisga'a Tribal Council asserted that the title to Nisga'a lands had never been extinguished. The case is significant because it was the first Supreme Court of Canada decision concerning Aboriginal rights in Canada, it used the Royal Proclamation in support of the claim, and it influenced the federal government's policy on negotiation. The six judges of the Supreme Court who heard the case were unanimous that Aboriginal rights did exist at the time of initial contact with Europeans. However, they were split evenly on whether those rights had subsequently been extinguished. The decision was significant enough that the federal government immediately changed its policy on dealing with Aboriginal rights from one of non-negotiation to one of negotiation. Thus, close to 100 years after the Nisga'a initiated their claim, in the mid-1970s the federal government finally agreed to enter into negotiations. It took considerably longer for the provincial government to join negotiations, but the Nisga'a were finally able to negotiate and implement a treaty in 2000 (see Part 6).

The *Sparrow* case is significant because it used the Constitution as an affirmation of Aboriginal rights. Ronald Sparrow, an elder of the Musqueam Nation in Vancouver, was charged and subsequently convicted of fishing with a drift net longer than legally permitted. In 1990 the Supreme Court of Canada overturned the conviction, ruling that the Constitution protected Aboriginal rights to fisheries. The court further ruled that any government regulations that infringe on those rights must be constitutionally justified, that Aboriginal rights are capable of evolving, that Aboriginal rights should be interpreted in a generous and liberal manner, and that the right of Aboriginal peoples to fish for food should be given priority over commercial and sport fishing.

The *Delgamuukw* case began in 1984 when thirty-five Gitxsan and Wet'suwet'en hereditary chiefs claimed ownership of their traditional territories, the right to self-government, and compensation for loss of lands and resources. In 1991, after three years of testimony, Chief Justice Allan McEachern of the Supreme Court of British Columbia ruled that Aboriginal rights had been extinguished during colonial times. The hereditary chiefs took the decision to the BC Court of Appeal, which ruled the Gitxsan and Wet'suwet'en did have Aboriginal rights but that those rights were non-exclusive. It recommended that the scope of the rights would best be determined through negotiation rather than litigation. The Gitxsan and Wet'suwet'en then took the case to the Supreme Court of

Canada, which in 1997 ordered a new trial and ruled on several issues arising in the case, including the nature of Aboriginal title and the rules for proving its existence. The Supreme Court of Canada also asserted that the lower courts should give more weight to oral histories of First Nations and that governments may infringe on Aboriginal title only if they have a "compelling and substantive legislative objective." Further, when governments do infringe thus, First Nations must receive "fair compensation."

Negotiations in the Late 1900s

Most First Nations in British Columbia never signed treaties. The exceptions are the fourteen treaties negotiated by Governor James Douglas on Vancouver Island in the early 1850s and Treaty 8, negotiated by the federal government in 1899. Treaty 8 dealt mostly with groups living in Alberta and the Northwest Territories but also included some nations from Saskatchewan and northeastern British Columbia.

Despite federal involvement in resolving the claims of the Nisga'a, the provincial government refused until 1990 to participate in negotiations with First Nations. From Joseph Trutch onward, spokespeople for the BC government either denied the existence of Aboriginal rights or declared that if Aboriginal rights did exist they were a federal responsibility. In 1990, however, the provincial government agreed to participate in the treaty-making process. Representatives of First Nations and the provincial and federal governments recommended establishing the British Columbia Claims Task Force to determine how negotiations should proceed. Key recommendations of the task force, implemented in 1992, were the creation of a six-stage process for negotiations and a treaty commission to oversee it.

The six-stage treaty negotiation process is as follows: a statement of intent by a First Nation to negotiate a treaty; preparations for negotiations; negotiation of a framework agreement; negotiation of an agreement-in-principle; negotiation to finalize a treaty; and implementation of the treaty. Many First Nations became involved in treaty negotiations, but the first modern-day treaty was not implemented until the twenty-first century (discussed in Part 6).

Anthropology in the Late 1900s

The nature of anthropological research began to change substantially in the late 1900s. In the 1970s large-scale development projects, coupled with heritage legislation, created a job market for archaeologists locating, assessing, and in some cases excavating archaeological sites. Initially, there was relatively little collaboration with First Nations, who often were not even made aware that archaeologists were looking for and in some cases excavating sites in the First Nations territories. Many First Nations were less than pleased that they were not consulted or asked for permission, and some established their own consultation and permitting systems in addition to the permit system of the provincial government.

While considerable work for archaeologists stemmed from legislation and development, First Nations also created a new avenue of archaeological research. When First Nations began court cases against governments and corporations, they had to document the use and occupancy of their territories and show cultural continuity in preparation for court, and some archaeologists became expert witnesses. Some First Nations also began their own archaeology programs. Similarly, archaeological work was undertaken in preparation for treaty negotiations.

Development projects also created work for cultural anthropologists. Governments often wanted to know what the impact of proposed large-scale development projects would be on First Nations of the area. This led to many cultural anthropologists undertaking traditional use studies, often abbreviated TUS, which usually focused on documenting the subsistence activities of First Nations and the importance of local resources to the group, especially economically.

The late 1900s also saw an increase in applied work for linguistic anthropologists, although this was much smaller in scale. This primarily involved working with First Nations to document their languages.

Recommended Readings and Resources

Many books on the history of British Columbia include substantial coverage of First Nations, including *Makuk: A New History of Aboriginal-White Relations*, by John Lutz (Vancouver: UBC Press, 2008), *The Pacific Province: A History of British Columbia*, edited by Hugh J.M. Johnston (Vancouver: Douglas and McIntyre, 1996), *Contact and Conflict: Indian-European Relations in British Columbia, 1774-1890*, by Robin Fisher (2nd ed., Vancouver: UBC Press, 1992), *Aboriginal Peoples and Politics: The Indian Land Question in British Columbia, 1849-1989*, by Paul Tennant (Vancouver: UBC Press, 1990), *Making Native Space: Colonialism, Resistance, and Reserves in British Columbia*, by Cole Harris (Vancouver: UBC Press, 2002), and *The Indian History of British Columbia*, Vol. 1, *The Impact of the White Man*, by Wilson Duff (Anthropology in British Columbia Memoir no. 5; Victoria: BC Provincial Museum, 1969).

Jean Barman provides some interesting details about the displacement of First Nations in Vancouver in *Stanley Park's Secret: The Forgotten Families of Whoi Whoi, Kanaka Ranch, and Brockton Point* (Madeira Park, BC: Harbour Publishing, 2005).

A good book on residential schools in Canada is *Shingwauk's Vision: A History of Native Residential Schools*, by J.R. Miller (Toronto: University of Toronto Press, 1996), and for the experiences of those attending in British Columbia in particular, *Resistance and Renewal: Surviving the Indian Residential School* by Celia Haig-Brown (Vancouver: Tillicum, 1988).

An Indigenous perspective on the impact of Europeans is provided by Kwakwaka'wakw member Gord Hill in *500 Years of Indigenous Resistance* (Oakland, CA: PM Press, 2009) and *The 500 Years of Resistance Comic Book* (Vancouver: Arsenal Pulp Press, 2010).

Although most academics are skeptical of a deliberate attempt at exterminating First Nations through smallpox, an alternative view is provided in *The True Story of Canada's "War" of Extermination on the Pacific*, by Tom Swanky (Burnaby, BC: Dragon Heart Enterprises, 2012).

Aboriginal Law Handbook, by Nancy Kleer et al. (4th ed., Toronto: Carswell, 2012), is a resource book on Canadian law and policy regarding First Nations and other Aboriginal peoples in Canada. *The Pleasure of the Crown: Anthropology, Law and First Nations*, by Dara Culhane (Vancouver: Talonbooks, 1998) includes lengthy commentary on the *Delgamuukw* case.

An excellent ethnography produced in the context of applied research in the late 1900s is *Maps and Dreams: Indians and the British Columbia Frontier*, by Hugh Brody (Vancouver: Douglas and McIntyre, 1988). Another very good book focusing on the experiences of First Nations is *The Burden of History: Colonialism and the Frontier Myth in a Rural Canadian Community*, by Elizabeth Furniss (Vancouver: UBC Press, 1999).

Part 6

First Nations and Anthropology
in the Twenty-First Century

Living in the Twenty-First Century

Compared to national averages, First Nations populations have fewer people complete high school and attend post-secondary institutions, higher rates of unemployment, significantly lower incomes even when working full-time, and lower life expectancy.

Traditional plant and animal resources are being depleted and water sources polluted. Access to traditional territories where subsistence, social, and spiritual activities occur is being cut off, and in some cases the lands and resources are being destroyed by mining and other resource-based industries.

Many First Nations people suffer the consequences of persistent and systemic racism, stereotypes, and misconceptions about their lives, cultures, and issues. Much of the adult population has suffered the consequences of the residential school system, with ongoing repercussions for family life.

Compared to other Canadians, the First Nations population is young. This is due to both higher rates of fertility and shorter life expectancy. Canada-wide, the proportion of First Nations under the age of fourteen is 28 percent, compared to only 17 percent of the non-Aboriginal population.

Despite the dour statistics on employment, education, health, and social conditions, however, trends indicate things are improving. Much of this can be attributed to First Nations taking more control of their own economies, as well as educational and social programs. The positive trend may also be attributed, at least in part, to increased advocacy through education, media, and politics, as well as asserting their rights.

Economic and Cultural Initiatives

First Nations economic initiatives have proliferated in British Columbia in recent years. In the tourism industry alone, for example, hundreds of businesses are owned and operated by First Nations people. Other industries in which First Nations have become competitive include, but are not limited to,

'Ksan. Many First Nations have taken control of the way they are represented, as illustrated by 'Ksan Historical Village and Museum, developed and operated by the Gitxsan. 'Ksan is located within Gitxsan territory, near Hazelton. *Courtesy of Thomas McIlwraith*

fishing, forestry, and land development. Some ventures are wholly owned and operated by one or more First Nations; others are operated in partnership with governments or private-sector companies.

Many First Nations have implemented programs in language, education, media, and health. Numerous programs have been devised to revitalize languages, and schools with First Nations teachers are now common on reserves. Various postsecondary First Nations institutes and programs have also been established, such as the Institute of Indigenous Government and the Nicola Valley Institute of Technology. Several First Nations and First Nations organizations have publishing programs producing high-quality educational and scholarly resources. Many First Nations have also founded cultural education centres, heritage parks, and museums.

Many First Nations have also been involved in initiatives to repatriate cultural and human remains. Tens of thousands of artifacts and hundreds of human skeletons have been removed from archaeological sites and taken from First Nations territories by anthropologists, collectors, and government agents. Many of these were taken unlawfully and have been stored in museums and private collections around the world. Some First Nations have been successful in getting skeletal remains returned for reburial and have built museums to house returned artifacts. The U'Mista Cultural Centre at Alert Bay, for example, was built primarily to house repatriated Kwakwaka'wakw items confiscated in the early twentieth century and stored in the Canadian Museum of Civilization.

Treaty Negotiations

The modern treaty process begun in the late 1900s has resulted in some treaties being implemented. The first modern-day treaty in British Columbia was the Nisga'a Treaty, implemented in 2000, which included about 2,000 square kilometres of land. The Tsawwassen First Nation Treaty, implemented in 2007, is the first urban treaty in British Columbia, and included approximately 724 acres of land. The Maa-nulth Treaty includes five First Nations – the Huu-ay-aht, the Ka:'yu:'k't'h'/Che:k:tles7et'h, the Toquaht, the Uchucklesaht, and the Ucluelet. It was implemented in 2011.

As of 2013, sixty First Nations were participating in treaty negotiations, some negotiating separately and others in groups, and representing about two-thirds of the First Nations population in British Columbia.

Outstanding Issues

Few people familiar with the last 200 years of BC history would argue that the First Nations people in the province have been treated fairly. Unfair dealings were certainly not unique to British Columbia, however, and in many ways were typical of the treatment Indigenous peoples received from colonizing nations throughout the world. Like Indigenous

Treaty Flakes (Breakfast Series), 2006. © Sonny Assu. *Artwork by Sonny Assu; image courtesy of the artist and the Equinox Gallery. Photo by Chris Meier*

peoples elsewhere, those in British Columbia are coming to terms with past economic, social, and legal injustices inflicted upon them. Some ways of dealing with those issues have included public education and apologies, government inquiries and commissions, the return of human remains and artifacts, and the ongoing treaty negotiation process. See Appendix 4 for the federal government's apology for its policy and practice of residential schools.

However, many federally recognized First Nations are not participating in treaty negotiations; consequently, approximately 30 percent of the registered Indian population is not represented in the process. Leadership of some First Nations have expressed no interest in participating in the negotiations using the existing framework, although they remain determined to assert their Aboriginal rights.

Another issue likely to become prominent is the treatment of non-status First Nations people. Although they have often suffered injustices equal to or greater than the ones inflicted on those with status, First Nations people without status are at a greater disadvantage. They will not benefit from treaty negotiations and have no avenue to address the same issues. Unlike the United States, Canada has no formal mechanism for groups to petition for status as a First Nation.

Asserting Rights and Identity

As in the past few hundred years, First Nations continue to assert their identity and rights in many ways, including protests, litigation, and negotiation. Since the late 1900s, rights are increasingly being asserted through media and public lectures. A new kind of leadership appears to be emerging among First Nations on issues relating to rights and other concerns; rather than chiefs and other elected officials, assertions of rights are now often led by young adults, frequently women.

Assertions of identity can be more subtle. One way has been to take control of terminology, including descriptors such as "First Nation," which was initiated by First Nations. Many First Nations people refuse to use terms such as "Aboriginal" and "Indian" because their use was largely initiated and has been sustained by governments. Similarly, many First Nations write the road signs in their territories in both English and their own languages. First Nations have changed their names, or the spelling of their names, to be more reflective of the names and pronunciations they use themselves. At public events, especially at places like large museums and educational institutions, First Nations people often provide a welcome in their own languages.

Assertions of identity are also expressed through art. Although revitalization of First Nations cultures has been ongoing since the 1960s, much of the revitalization has gone public only recently. It is now common, for example, for First Nations to invite the public to cultural events and displays. Traditional ceremonies at the raising of totem poles or unveiling of sculptures, wherever they may be, allow artists to provide a First Nations context and meaning to the public. A concern for many First Nations across the continent is the appropriation of their identities and cultures by others, especially in regard to such things as names and mascots for sports teams. In British Columbia there is concern about the appropriation of stories, arts and crafts, and cultural or intellectual property rights, such as medicinal uses of plants. In some cases, non-First Nations people have recorded – thus acquiring copyright – on First Nations stories. Similarly, some non-First Nations people have appropriated images from rock art, leading to applications by First Nations for trademarks on rock art designs. First Nations and Native American arts and crafts is a billion-dollar industry in North America, and estimates indicate that almost all the jewellery sold and about half the arts and crafts are created and manufactured by non-Indigenous people. In the United States, the Indian Arts and Crafts Act prohibits non-Native Americans from claiming their products are authentic. Many would like a similar law in British Columbia.

First Nations and Anthropology in the Twenty-First Century

The changes in anthropology focusing on First Nations that began in the late 1900s are ongoing. Archaeologists continue to work in advance of resource development, and also share information afterward with First Nations. Thousands of archaeological sites continue to be added to the inventory.

While cultural anthropologists still conduct traditional, research-based ethnographic work, there has been a growth in applied work assessing potential impacts of development projects on communities, as well as for court cases and treaty negotiations. Traditional use studies still occur, and governments and corporations seem to prefer them because they are more easily translated into dollars. Increasingly, however, anthropologists are focusing on traditional ecological knowledge, often abbreviated TEK. Whereas traditional use studies usually apply categories of information important to scientists, government, and corporations, research on traditional ecological knowledge frames data collection in categories important to First Nations and often ties in their knowledge and use of environmental resources with spirituality, morals, oral tradition, intuition, and other elements of culture.

The Pizza Test

A common misconception is that First Nations cultures somehow become inauthentic once the people start incorporating elements of other cultures, and that First Nations claims of identity and rights are therefore without foundation. In a sense, the argument is that Aboriginal rights and identity are given up once First Nations begin to participate in modern culture.

To First Nations people, anthropologists, and many others, this notion is nonsense. No culture, First Nations or otherwise, is static or unchanging. Almost every aspect of every culture originated from somewhere else. A Canadian is not less Canadian because he or she drinks coffee, wears cotton clothing, and uses computers, although none of those things was invented in Canada. Many who believe that First Nations cultures are inauthentic seem to think that in order to have rights, First Nations people must live as their ancestors did before the arrival of Europeans in the area. But First Nations cultures in the twenty-first century are no less authentic than other cultures.

First Nations people are challenged – in media, on the public stage, and in court – on their authenticity based on how they live in contemporary times. Anthropologist Robin Ridington

First Nations Cultures Still Exist

One of the most perplexing challenges that First Nations and anthropologists have to deal with is the notion that because First Nations adopt elements of non-Indigenous cultures, First Nations cultures are no longer authentic. The idea that adopting elements of other cultures has extinguished First Nations culture is nonsense to most First Nations and anthropologists. Anthropologists know that almost all elements of all cultures are borrowed. Adopting new technologies, altering customs, and incorporating Christianity into traditional belief systems does not mean a First Nations culture is not authentic. Very few First Nations people want to fully assimilate into Euro-Canadian society. For most First

("Re-Creation in Canadian First Nation Literatures: 'When You Sing It Now, Just Like New,'" *Anthropologica* 43, 2 [2001]: 223-24) describes what has come to be known as the pizza test:

Oral tradition has it that in a case involving the demonstration of aboriginal rights by a First Nations group, lawyers for the Crown asked a plaintiff about what foods she ate: fish, moosemeat, berries, grease – "Yes." Then came the clincher. What about pizza? "Well, yes, I eat pizza sometimes." Voila! The lawyer argued that she could no longer claim aboriginal rights because pizza is not an authentic aboriginal dish. This argument has entered a folklore shared by participants in land claims issues as "the pizza test."

Anthropologists should shoulder some of the blame for failing to educate people about the nature of cultures – the fact that all cultures are always changing. It should be clearly understood that eating pizza, driving trucks, or using outboard motors and cell phones does not mean First Nations cultures are not authentic. The core elements of the cultures remain.

Arthur Nole of the Iskut First Nation at a lookout, scanning for moose and caribou near the headwaters of the Skeena River. *Courtesy of Thomas McIlwraith*

Iskut camp. Many First Nations maintain elements of their traditional cultures, including food-gathering activities. This camp, known as Kati Cho, has been used on an annual basis by members of the Iskut Nation for hundreds, and perhaps thousands, of years. *Courtesy of Thomas McIlwraith; reproduced with permission of the Iskut Nation*

Nations, the core of their cultures remains despite change. Whether hunting with pickup trucks and rifles, or fishing with boats and outboard motors, First Nations people are still maintaining their traditional lifeways.

It is also important to understand that people can be part of more than one culture. In a sense, many First Nations people live in two worlds – that of their home community and that of Canadian society. This is especially the case for people who live primarily in an urban area but often return to their traditional territories. First Nations people often negotiate their identities depending on context. This does not make their cultures, lifeways, practices, and experiences any less authentic.

Reconciling Pickup Trucks and Rifles in First Nations Cultures

The traditional territories of the Iskut First Nation are in the northwest interior of British Columbia. Part of the larger group commonly known as Tahltan, the Iskut population numbers about 700. Some non-First Nations people challenge Iskut cultural authenticity since they hunt with modern technologies. But adopting modern technologies does not make the tradition of hunting any less vital to Iskut culture.

Anthropologist Thomas McIlwraith has spent considerable time researching and living among the Iskut in the early twenty-first century. In *"We Are Still Didene": Stories of Hunting and History from Northern British Columbia* (Toronto: University of Toronto Press, 2012), he relates a story told by an Iskut elder, Arthur Nole.

Arthur Nole was speaking in the Tahltan language to a group of seven- and eight-year-olds at the Iskut school, ostensibly to help preserve the stories and language and develop curriculum materials. He described how in the past the ancestors often had to travel far on foot to hunt moose, and then after they killed a moose, they packed it out by themselves and with dogs. He finished the story by saying that today they use vehicles, but they are still *didene* (Native people).

McIlwraith's analysis of Arthur Nole's story has much to say about Iskut culture, including hunting, the use of modern technology, and challenges to authenticity:

> Arthur speaks about changes to hunting practices while affirming a Native heritage. By doing so, he challenges non-Iskut people – trophy hunters, government bureaucrats, and non-Natives in the nearby towns of Tatl'ah and Terrace – whom Natives have heard asking how one can reconcile the use of tools such as trucks and rifles with a tradition of hunting for food. Arthur's words establish a connection between past hunting practices, such as walking, and the use of current technologies, such as vehicles. And his comments contain an underlying political sentiment: adaptation to and acceptance of cultural change are reasonable and clever ... Arthur's story exemplifies overlapping orientations in the lives of Iskut Villagers ... In talk, story, and action, Iskut people debate about the apparent opposition of participating in a sustenance hunting culture and working for a wage – and what those mean for remaining *didene*. On the one hand they speak with enthusiasm and pride about hunting and food animals and continue to hunt with interest and intensity. On the other hand, almost all of them work in the Canadian wage-based and industrial economy, and they value wage work highly for the material rewards it makes possible ... They easily reconcile hunting with the wage work that, in most cases, allows them to continue hunting ... It is outsiders, non-Natives typically, who sometimes assert that Iskut people should not operate in the two worlds of sustenance hunting and capitalism. Modernization and acculturation are one-way processes, they claim ... Arthur sees the use of vehicles in a hunt as being consistent with being *didene*, a Native person; hunting is a current and worthwhile activity. (6-7)

Summit Lake, Sekani Territory. Bernie Chingee, Sekani, patrols for fish and moose in his ancestral lands north of Prince George. *Courtesy of Thomas McIlwraith*

Final Comments: Things to Remember

This isn't a long, comprehensive, or dense book, but the information presented is still a lot to remember. Following is what I hope all readers can retain for years to come, and hopefully pass on to others.

1 The First Nations peoples and cultures of British are extremely diverse. Labels have specific meanings. If uncertain about which term to use, "First Nation" is a good default.
2 Not all First Nations are registered Indians or members of a particular band or nation; nor are most of those identifying as First Nation exempt from paying taxes, or entitled to free housing, gas, and postsecondary education.
3 "First Nation" has multiple meanings. It can be used as an adjective, as in "a First Nations person," and it can also be used as a noun, to refer to a political, social, linguistic, or ethnic grouping.

4 No single group or leader represents the interests of all First Nations people and cultures in the province.

5 First Nations have a very long and well-documented past, including the physical evidence of tens of thousands of archaeological sites and millions of artifacts.

6 It is against the law to disturb an archaeological site without a permit.

7 Colonialism had devastating impacts on First Nations populations and cultures.

8 First Nations are extremely resilient.

9 First Nations cultures in the twenty-first century are authentic.

10 British Columbia anthropology has been intricately linked with First Nations.

Recommended Readings and Resources

What this book does for the First Nations of British Columbia, *The Indigenous Peoples of North America: A Concise Anthropological Overview* by Robert Muckle (Toronto: University of Toronto Press, 2012) does for the Indigenous peoples in all of Canada and the United States. For those wishing a more comprehensive anthropological view of the Indigenous peoples of North America, *A Companion to the Anthropology of North American Indians*, edited by Thomas Biolsi (Malden, MA: Blackwell, 2008), is recommended.

An excellent ethnography of a First Nation (Iskut) in contemporary times is *"We Are Still Didene": Stories of Hunting and History from Northern British Columbia*, by Thomas McIlwraith (Toronto: University of Toronto Press, 2012). *Spirits of Our Whaling Ancestors: Revitalizing Makah and Nuu-chah-nulth Traditions*, by Charlotte Cote (Seattle: University of Washington Press, 2010), is an equally excellent book by a Nuu'chah'nulth scholar writing about First Nations in contemporary times.

For those wishing further background on Aboriginal rights and anthropology, *Applied Anthropology in Canada: Understanding Aboriginal Issues*, by Edward Hedican (2nd ed., Toronto: University of Toronto Press, 2008) and *Ending Denial: Understanding Aboriginal Issues*, by Wayne Warry (Toronto: University of Toronto Press, 2008) are recommended.

Appendices

Appendix 1
The First Nations of British Columbia

This appendix identifies all the federally recognized First Nations in British Columbia. The list includes some First Nations primarily based in the Yukon or Northwest Territories that consider part of the province as including some of their traditional territory. Most First Nations listed here are commonly considered to be part of a larger ethnic group, as outlined in Appendix 2.

The primary listings here follow the names and spellings in the register maintained by Aboriginal Affairs and Northern Development Canada as of 2013. The number in parentheses following the name of the First Nation is the number assigned by the federal government. Knowing the number may alleviate confusion due to name and spelling changes. Symbols such as punctuation marks and numbers represent sounds that cannot be reproduced accurately with the English alphabet alone. Pronunciations are taken from a variety of sources, including guides published by the federal government, the provincial government, and the Assembly of First Nations.

The names and spellings of First Nations continue to change. There is often inconsistency in the names and spellings of First Nations used by the federal government, provincial government, First Nations organizations, and First Nations themselves. Therefore this list is not definitive.

ʔAkisq'nuk (604)
Pronounced "a-kiss-qe-nuk." Sometimes known as Akisq'nuk. Formerly known as Columbia Lake. Traditional territories and reserves in southeastern British Columbia.

ʔEsdilagh *(709)*
Pronounced "ess-dey-la." Formerly known as Alexandria.
Traditional territories and reserves in the central interior.

Acho Dene Koe (758)
Based primarily in the Northwest Territories but claim
traditional territory in British Columbia.

Adams Lake (684)
Traditional territories and reserves in the southern interior.

Ahousaht (659)
Pronounced "a-house-sat" or "a-howz-at." Traditional
territories and reserves on and around the west coast of
Vancouver Island.

Aitchelitz (558)
Pronounced "a-che-leets." Traditional territories and
reserves in the Fraser Valley region of southwestern
British Columbia.

Alexandria. See *ʔEsdilagh.*

Alexis Creek (710)
Traditional territories and reserves in central British
Columbia.

Alkali Lake. See *Esk'etemc.*

Anaham. See *Tl'etinqox-t'in.*

Ashcroft (685)
Traditional territories and reserves in the southern
interior, near Ashcroft.

Atlin. See *Taku River Tlingit.*

Babine. See *Nat'oot'en.*

Beecher Bay (640)
Also known as Scia'new. Traditional territories and
reserves on Vancouver Island.

Bella Bella. See *Heiltsuk.*

Bella Coola. See *Nuxalk.*

Blueberry River (547)
Traditional territories and reserves in northeastern
British Columbia.

Bonaparte (686)
   Traditional territories and reserves in the southern interior, near Cache Creek.
Boothroyd (700)
   Traditional territories and reserves in the southern interior.
Boston Bar (701)
   Traditional territories and reserves in the southern interior.
Bridge River (590)
   Traditional territories and reserves in the southern interior.
Broman Lake. See *Wet'suwet'en.*
Burns Lake (619)
   Traditional territories and reserves in central British Columbia.
Burrard. See *Tsleil-Waututh.*
Campbell River (622)
   Also known as We Wai Kum. Traditional territories and reserves near Campbell River on Vancouver Island.
Canim Lake (713)
   Also known as Tsq'escen. Traditional territories and reserves in the southern interior.
Canoe Creek. See *Stswecem'c Xgat'tem.*
Cape Mudge (623)
   Also known as We Wai Kai. Traditional territories and reserves around Campbell River and the northern Gulf Islands.
Carcross/Tagish (491)
   Based primarily in Yukon but claim traditional territory in northern British Columbia.
Cayoose Creek (591)
   Pronounced "kiy-oos." Traditional territories and reserves in the southern interior.
Champagne and Aishihik (493)
   Based in Yukon and northern British Columbia.

Chawathil (583)

Pronounced "shi-wath-il." Formerly known as Hope. Traditional territories and reserves located in southern British Columbia, near Hope.

Cheam (584)

Pronounced "chee-am." Traditional territories and reserves located in southern British Columbia, near Rosedale.

Chehalis. See *Sts'ailes.*

Chemainus. See *Stz'uminus.*

Cheslatta Carrier (620)

Traditional territories and reserves in the central interior, near Burns Lake.

Clayoquat (pronounced "clay-kwot"). See *Tla-o-qui-aht.*

Coldwater (693)

Traditional territories and reserves in the southern interior, near Merritt.

Columbia Lake. See *ʔAkisq'nuk.*

Comox. See *K'omoks.*

Cook's Ferry (694)

Traditional territories and reserves in the southern interior, near Spences Bridge.

Coquitlam. See *Kwikwetlem.*

Cowichan (642)

Pronounced "cow-ut-zun." Traditional territories and reserves on Vancouver Island.

Cowichan Lake. See *Lake Cowichan.*

Da'naxda'xw (635)

Pronounced "da-nuk-dah." Formerly known as Tanakteuk. Traditional territories and reserves near Alert Bay.

Deadman's Creek. See *Skeetchestn.*

Dease River (504)

Traditional territories and reserves in northeastern British Columbia.

Denetsaa Tse Tse K'Nai. See *Prophet River.*

Ditidaht (662)

Pronounced "dee-tee-dot" or "dee-tee-dat." Traditional territories and reserves on and around the west coast of Vancouver Island.

Doig River (548)

Traditional territories and reserves in northeastern British Columbia.

Douglas (561)

Traditional territories and reserves in the southern interior.

Dzawada'enuxw (636)

Formerly known as Tsawataineuk. Traditional territories and reserves on the central coast of British Columbia, near Kingcome Inlet.

Ehattesaht (634)

Pronounced "eh-hat-eh-sat." Traditional territories and reserves on and around the west coast of Vancouver Island.

Esk'etemc (711)

Pronounced "es-KET-em." Formerly known as Alkali Lake. Traditional territories and reserves in central British Columbia.

Esquimalt (644)

Pronounced "ess-KWY-malt." Traditional territories and reserves on and around southern Vancouver Island.

Fort George. See *Lheidli T'enneh.*

Fort Nelson (543)

Traditional territories and reserves in northern British Columbia.

Fort Ware. See *Kwadacha.*

Fountain. See *Xaxli'p.*

Fraser Lake. See *Nadleh Whut'en.*

Gitanmaax (531)

Traditional territories and reserves in northwestern British Columbia.

Gitanyow (537)
Pronounced "GIT-an-yow." Traditional territories and reserves in northwestern British Columbia.

Gitga'at (675)
Pronounced "GIT-gat." Traditional territories and reserves in northwestern British Columbia.

Gitsegukla (535)
Pronounced "GIT-zee-gee-u-kla." Traditional territories and reserves in northwestern British Columbia.

Gitwangak (536)
Pronounced "GIT-win-gah." Traditional territories and reserves in northwestern British Columbia.

Gitxaala (672)
Pronounced "GHEET-h-khat-la." Formerly known as Kitkatla. Traditional territories and reserves in northwestern British Columbia.

Glen Vowell (533)
Traditional territories and reserves in northwestern British Columbia.

Gwa'sala-Nakwaxda'xw (724)
Pronounced "gwas-sala nak-wah-dah." Formerly known as Tsulquate. Traditional territories and reserves on northern Vancouver Island and the central mainland coast.

Gwawaenuk (627)
Traditional territories and reserves along the central coast.

Hagwilget (534)
Traditional territories and reserves in northwestern British Columbia.

Haisla (676)
Pronounced "hyzlah." Also known as Kitimat or Kitamaat. Traditional territories and reserves on the central mainland coast.

Halalt (645)
Traditional territories and reserves on southern Vancouver Island.

Halfway River (546)
Traditional territories and reserves in northeastern British Columbia.

Heiltsuk (538)
Pronounced "HAIL-tsuk." Formerly known as Bella Bella. Traditional territories and reserves on the central coast.

Hesquiaht (661)
Pronounced "HESS-kwee-at." Traditional territories and reserves on and around the west coast of Vancouver Island.

High Bar (703)
Traditional territories and reserves in south-central British Columbia.

Homalco (552)
Pronounced "hoe-mall-co." Also known as Xwemalhkwu. Traditional territories and reserves on northern Vancouver Island and the central mainland coast.

Hope. See Chawathil.

Hupacasath (664)
Pronounced "who-petch-ah-set." Formerly known as Opetchesaht. Traditional territories and reserves on the west coast of Vancouver Island.

Huu-ay-aht (663)
Pronounced "hoo-EYE-at" or "hoo-AY-at." Also known as Ohiaht. Traditional territories and reserves on Vancouver Island.

Iskut (683)
Pronounced "iss-kut." Traditional territories and reserves in northwestern British Columbia.

Kamloops. See Tk'emlups te Secwepemc.

Kanaka Bar (704)
Traditional territories and reserves in the southern interior.

Katzie (563)
Pronounced "KUT-zee" or "kate-zee." Traditional territories and reserves in the Fraser Valley region of southwestern British Columbia.

Ka:'yu:'k't'h'/Che:k:tles7et'h' (638)
Pronounced "ky-YOU-cut." Formerly Kyoquot.
Traditional territories and reserves on and around the
west coast of Vancouver Island.

Kispiox (532)
Pronounced "KISS-pee-ox." Traditional territories and
reserves in northwestern British Columbia.

Kitasoo (540)
Pronounced "kit-AH-soo." Also known as Klemtu.
Traditional territories and reserves in northwestern
British Columbia.

Kitimat, Kitamaat. See *Haisla.*

Kitkatla. See *Gitxaala.*

Kitselas (680)
Pronounced "git-SEL-as." Traditional territories and
reserves in northwestern British Columbia.

Kitsumkalum (681)
Traditional territories and reserves in northwestern
British Columbia.

Klahoose (553)
Pronounced "kla-HOOS." Traditional territories and
reserves around Cortez Island and nearby mainland
coastal areas.

Klemtu. See *Kitasoo.*

Kluskus (721)
Traditional territories and reserves in central British
Columbia.

K'omoks (624)
Also known as Comox. Traditional territories and reserves
on and around the central east coast of Vancouver Island.

Kwadacha (610)
Also known as Fort Ware. Traditional territories and
reserves in central British Columbia.

Kwakiutl (626)
Traditional territories and reserves in central coastal areas.

Kwantlen (564)
Traditional territories and reserves in the Fraser Valley region of southwestern British Columbia.

Kwaw-kwaw-Apilt (580)
Pronounced "kwa-kwa-a-pilt." Traditional territories and reserves in the Fraser Valley region of southwestern British Columbia.

Kwiakah (628)
Pronounced "KWEE-kah." Traditional territories and reserves on northern Vancouver Island and the central mainland coast region.

Kwicksutaineuk-ah-kwaw-ah-mish (625)
Pronounced "kweek-soo-tain-an-kwa-a-meesh." Traditional territories and reserves on Vancouver Island.

Kwikwetlem (560)
Formerly known as Coquitlam. Traditional territories and reserves in southwestern British Columbia, near Coquitlam.

Kyoquot. See *Ka:'yu:'k't'h'/Che:k:tles7et'h'.*

Lakahahmen. See *Leq'á:mel.*

Lake Cowichan (643)
Also known as Cowichan Lake. Traditional territories and reserves on Vancouver Island.

Lax-Kw'alaams (674)
Pronounced "la-kwa-lahms." Traditional territories and reserves in northwestern British Columbia.

Leq'á:mel (579)
Pronounced "la-camel." Also known as Leq'amel and Lakahahmen. Traditional territories and reserves in the Fraser Valley region of southwestern British Columbia.

Lheit-Lit'en. See *Lheidli T'enneh.*

Lheidli T'enneh (611)
Pronounced "klate-lee ten-eh." Also known as Lheit-Lit'en, and formerly Fort George. Traditional territories and reserves in central British Columbia.

Lhtako Dene (715)
Formerly known as Red Bluff. Traditional territories and reserves in central British Columbia.

Lillooet. See T'it'q'et.

Lil'wat. See Mount Currie.

Little Shuswap Lake (689)
Traditional territories and reserves in the southern interior.

Lower Kootenay (606)
Traditional territories and reserves in the Kootenay region of southeastern British Columbia.

Lower Nicola (695)
Traditional territories and reserves in the southern interior, near Merritt.

Lower Similkameen (598)
Traditional territories and reserves in the southern interior.

Lyackson (646)
Pronounced "lay-ik-sen." Traditional territories and reserves on and around Valdez Island, off the east coast of Vancouver Island.

Lytton (705)
Traditional territories and reserves in the southern interior, near Lytton.

Malahat (647)
Pronounced "malah-hat." Traditional territories and reserves on southern Vancouver Island.

Mamalilikulla-Qwe'Qwa'Sot'Em (629)
Pronounced "mamma-leel-eh-quala-quee-qwa-soot-ee-nuk." Traditional territories and reserves in the central coast region.

Matsqui (565)
Pronounced "mat-squee." Traditional territories and reserves in the Fraser Valley region of southwestern British Columbia.

McLeod Lake (618)
Traditional territories and reserves in central British Columbia.

Metlakatla (673)
Traditional territories and reserves in the north coast region.

Moricetown (530)
Traditional territories and reserves in north-central British Columbia.

Mount Currie (557)
Also known as Lil'wat. Traditional territories in southern British Columbia, near Pemberton.

Mowachat/Muchalaht (630)
Traditional territories and reserves on and around the west coast of Vancouver Island.

Musqueam (550)
Pronounced "MUSS-quee-um." Traditional territories and reserves in and around Vancouver.

Nadleh Whut'en (612)
Pronounced "nad-lay woo-ten." Also known as Fraser Lake. Traditional territories and reserves in north-central British Columbia.

Nak'azdli (614)
Pronounced "na-k-ahz-dlee." Also known as Necoslie. Traditional territories and reserves in northern British Columbia, near Fort St. James.

Namgis (631)
Pronounced "NOM-gees." Formerly known as Nimpkish. Traditional territories and reserves near Alert Bay.

Nanaimo. See *Snuneymuxw.*

Nanoose (649)
Traditional territories and reserve on the east coast of Vancouver Island.

Nat'oot'en (607)
Formerly known as Babine and Lake Babine. Traditional territories in north-central British Columbia.

Nazko (720)
Pronounced "NAZ-koh." Traditional territories and reserves in central British Columbia.

Necoslie. See Nak'azdli.

Nee-Tahi-Buhn (726)
Pronounced "nee-tahee-boon." Traditional territories and reserves in central British Columbia, west of Prince George.

Neskonlith (690)
Traditional territories and reserves in the southern interior.

New Westminster (566)
Also known as Qayqayt. Traditional territory and reserve in southwestern British Columbia, near New Westminster.

Nicomen (696)
Traditional territories and reserves in the southern interior.

Nimpkish. See Namgis.

Nisga'a Village of Gingolx (671)
Pronounced "gin-GOL-ch." Traditional territories in northwestern British Columbia.

Nisga'a Village of Gitwinksihlkw (679)
Pronounced "git-win-k-shisq." Traditional territories in northwestern British Columbia.

Nisga'a Village of Laxgalt'sap (678)
Pronounced "lak-al-zap." Traditional territories in northwestern British Columbia.

Nisga'a Village of New Aiyansh (677)
Traditional territories in northwestern British Columbia.

Nooaitch (699)
Pronounced "noo-eye-ch." Traditional territories and reserves in the southern interior.

North Thompson. See Simpcw.

N'Quatqua (556)

Formerly known as Anderson Lake. Traditional territories and reserves in southern British Columbia.

Nuchatlaht (639)

Pronounced "noo-HAT-lat." Traditional territories and reserves on and around the west coast of Vancouver Island.

Nuwitti. See *Tlatlasikwala.*

Nuxalk (539)

Pronounced "NOO-hulk." Formerly known as Bella Coola. Traditional territories and reserves on the central coast of British Columbia.

Ohamil. See *Shxw'ow'hamel.*

Ohiaht. See *Huu-ay-aht.*

Okanagan (616)

Traditional territories and reserves in the Okanagan region of southern British Columbia, near Vernon.

Old Massett Village Council (669)

Traditional territories and reserves on Haida Gwaii.

Opetchesaht. See *Hupacasath.*

Oregon Jack Creek (692)

Traditional territories and reserves in the southern interior.

Osoyoos (596)

Pronounced "o-soy-use." Traditional territories and reserves in the Okanagan region of southern British Columbia.

Oweekeno/Wuikinuxv Nation (541)

Pronounced "o-wik-en-o." Traditional territories and reserves in the central coastal region of British Columbia.

Pacheedaht (658)

Pronounced "pah-chee-da." Traditional territories and reserves on Vancouver Island.

Pauquachin (658)
Pronounced "pak-quw-chin." Traditional territories and reserves on Vancouver Island.

Pavilion. See *Ts'kw'aylaxw.*

Penelakut (650)
Pronounced "pen-EL-ah-kut." Traditional territories and reserves in southwestern British Columbia, including the Gulf Islands.

Penticton (597)
Traditional territories and reserves in the Okanagan region of southern British Columbia.

Peters (586)
Traditional territories and reserves in the Fraser Valley region of southern British Columbia, near Hope.

Popkum (585)
Traditional territories and reserves in the Fraser Valley region of southwest British Columbia, near Chilliwack.

Prophet River (544)
Also known as Denetsaa Tse Tse K'Nai. Traditional territories and reserves in northern British Columbia, near Fort Nelson.

Qayqayt (pronounced "kee-kite"). See *New Westminster.*

Qualicum (651)
Pronounced "KWAH-lik-uhm." Traditional territories and reserve on the east coast of Vancouver Island.

Quatsino (633)
Pronounced "kwat-seeno." Traditional territories and reserves on northern Vancouver Island.

Red Bluff. See *Lhtako Dene.*

Saik'uz (615)
Pronounced "sake-ooz." Formerly known as Stony Creek. Traditional territories and reserves in central British Columbia.

Samahquam (567)
Pronounced "sam-ah-kwam." Traditional territories and reserves in the southern interior.

Saulteau (542)
Pronounced "saul-toe." Traditional territories and reserves in northeastern British Columbia.

Scia'new. See *Beecher Bay.*

Scowlitz (568)
Pronounced "scow-litz." Traditional territories and reserves in the Fraser Valley region of southwestern British Columbia.

Seabird Island (581)
Traditional territories and reserves in the Fraser Valley region of southwestern British Columbia.

Sechelt (551)
Pronounced "SEA-shelt." Also known as Shishalh. Traditional territories and "band lands" on the south coastal mainland of British Columbia, north of Vancouver.

Semiahmoo (569)
Traditional territories and reserves in southwestern British Columbia.

Seton Lake (595)
Traditional territories and reserves in southern British Columbia.

Shackan (698)
Pronounced "shah-ken." Traditional territories and reserves in southern British Columbia.

Shishalh. See *Sechelt.*

Shuswap (605)
Pronounced "shoe-swap." Traditional territories and reserves in the southern interior.

Shxwha:y Village (570)
Pronounced "sh-why." Formerly Skway. Traditional territories and reserves in the Fraser Valley regions of southwestern British Columbia.

Shxw'ow'hamel (587)

Pronounced "sh-wow-HA-mel." Also known as Ohamil. Traditional territories and reserves in southern British Columbia.

Simpcw (691)

Pronounced "simp-qwuh." Also known as North Thompson. Traditional territories and reserves in the southern interior.

Siska (706)

Pronounced "sis-kah." Traditional territories and reserves in the southern interior.

Skatin (562)

Pronounced "skah-teen." Traditional territories and reserves in southern British Columbia.

Skawahlook (582)

Pronounced "skwa-ha-look." Traditional territories and reserves in the Fraser Valley region of southwestern British Columbia.

Skeetchestn (687)

Pronounced "skeet-ch-sin." Formerly known as Deadman's Creek. Traditional territories and reserves in the southern interior.

Skidegate (670)

Traditional territories and reserves on Haida Gwaii.

Skin Tyee (729)

Traditional territories and reserves in west-central British Columbia.

Skowkale (571)

Pronounced "sko-kale." Traditional territories and reserves in the Fraser Valley region of southwestern British Columbia.

Skuppah (707)

Traditional territories and reserves in the southern interior.

Skwah (573)
Traditional territories and reserves in the Fraser Valley region of southwestern British Columbia.

Skway. See *Shxwha:y Village.*

Sliammon (554)
Pronounced "SLIGH-am-un." Also known as Tla'amin. Traditional territories in the south coastal region of British Columbia, around Powell River.

Snuneymuxw (648)
Pronounced "snoo-NAI-muk" or "snuh-NAY-mow." Also known as Nanaimo. Traditional territories on and around the east-central coast of Vancouver Island.

Soda Creek (716)
Traditional territories and reserves in central British Columbia.

Songhees (656)
Traditional territories and reserves on and around southeastern Vancouver Island.

Sooke. See *T'Sou-ke.*

Soowahlie (572)
Pronounced "soo-wall-ee." Traditional territories and reserves in the Fraser Valley region of southwestern British Columbia.

Spallumcheen. See *Splatsin.*

Splatsin (600)
Formerly known as Spallumcheen. Traditional territories and reserves in the southern interior.

Spuzzum (708)
Traditional territories and reserves in the Fraser Canyon region of southwestern British Columbia.

Squamish (555)
Pronounced "SKWA-mish." Traditional territories and reserves in southwestern British Columbia.

Squiala (574)
Pronounced "skwye-ala." Traditional territories and

reserves in the Fraser Valley region of southwestern British Columbia.

St. Mary's (602)
Traditional territories and reserves in southeastern British Columbia.

Stellat'en (613)
Pronounced "stell-at-in." Traditional territories and reserves in central British Columbia, west of Prince George.

Stone. See Yunesit'in.

Stony Creek. See Saik'uz.

Sts'ailes (559)
Formerly known as Chehalis. Traditional territories and reserves in the Fraser Valley region of southwestern British Columbia.

Stswecem'c Xgat'tem (723)
Formerly Canoe Creek. Traditional territories and reserves in the southern interior.

Stz'uminus (641)
Also known as Chemainus. Traditional territories and reserves in the south coastal region, including southern Vancouver Island and the Gulf Islands.

Sumas (578)
Traditional territories and reserve in the Fraser Valley region of southwestern British Columbia, near Abbotsford.

Tahltan (682)
Pronounced "tall-tan." Traditional territories and reserves in northeastern British Columbia, near Telegraph Creek.

Takla Lake (608)
Pronounced "tack-lah." Traditional territories and reserves in central British Columbia.

Taku River Tlingit (501)
Also known as Atlin. Territories and reserves in north-western British Columbia.

Tanakteuk. See Da'naxda'xw.

T'it'q'et (593)
Pronounced "tlee-tl-cut." Also known as Lillooet. Traditional territories and reserves in the southern interior.

Tk'emlups te Secwepemc (688)
Also known as Kamloops. Traditional territories and reserves in the southern interior.

Tla'amin. See *Sliammon.*

Tla-o-qui-aht (660)
Also known as Clayoquat. Traditional territories and reserves on and around the west coast of Vancouver Island.

Tlatlasikwala (632)
Pronounced "tla-tla-see-kwa-la." Formerly known as Nuwitti. Traditional territories and reserves on northern Vancouver Island and the coastal mainland region.

Tl'azt'en (617)
Traditional territories and reserves in north-central British Columbia.

Tl'etinqox-t'in (712)
Pronounced "clay-teen-co-teen." Formerly known as Anaham. Traditional territories and reserves in central British Columbia.

Tlowitsis (637)
Pronounced "tla-oe-was-zees." Formerly known as Turnour Island. Traditional territories and reserves in the central coast region.

Tobacco Plains (603)
Traditional territories and reserves in southeastern British Columbia, near Cranbrook.

Toosey (718)
Traditional territories and reserves in central British Columbia.

Toquaht (666)
Pronounced "toe-quat." Traditional territories on and around the west coast of Vancouver Island.

Tsartlip (653)
Pronounced "sart-lip." Traditional territories and reserves
in the south coastal region, including the Gulf Islands.

Tsawataineuk. See *Dzawada'enuxw.*

Tsawout (654)
Pronounced "tsa-woot." Traditional territories and
reserves in the south coastal region, including the Gulf
Islands.

Tsawwassen (577)
Pronounced "tah-WASS-en." Traditional territory in the
south coast mainland region.

Tsay Keh Dene (609)
Pronounced "say keh de-NEH." Traditional territories
and reserves in central British Columbia.

Tseshaht (665)
Pronounced "tse-shat" or "say-shot." Traditional territories
and reserves on Vancouver Island.

Tseycum (655)
Pronounced "tsay-kum." Traditional territories and
reserves in the south coastal region, including southeastern Vancouver Island and the Gulf Islands.

Ts'kw'aylaxw (594)
Pronounced "TS-KWHY-lux." Also known as Pavilion.
Traditional territories and reserves in the southern
interior.

Tsleil-Waututh (549)
Pronounced "TSLAY-wah-tooth." Also known as Burrard.
Traditional territories in the southwestern mainland
area.

T'Sou-ke (657)
Pronounced "sook." Also known as Sooke. Traditional
territories and reserves on Vancouver Island.

Tsq'escen. See *Canim Lake.*

Tsulquate. See *Gwa'sala-Nakwaxda'xw.*

Turnour Island. See *Tlowitsis.*

Tzeachten (575)
Pronounced "chak-tun." Traditional territories and reserves in the Fraser River Valley region of southwestern British Columbia.

Uchucklesaht (667)
Pronounced "u-CHUK-le-sat." Traditional territories and reserves on Vancouver Island.

Ucluelet (668)
Pronounced "you-CLUE-let." Also known as Yuułuʔiłʔatḥ. Traditional territories and reserves on and around the west coast of Vancouver Island.

Ulkatcho (722)
Pronounced "ul-gat-cho." Traditional territories and reserves in central British Columbia.

Union Bar (588)
Traditional territories and reserves in southern British Columbia, north of Hope.

Upper Nicola (697)
Traditional territories and reserves in the southern interior, near Merritt.

Upper Similkameen (599)
Traditional territories and reserves in southern British Columbia.

We Wai Kai. See *Cape Mudge.*

We Wai Kum. See *Campbell River.*

West Moberly (545)
Traditional territories and reserves in northeastern British Columbia.

Westbank (601)
Traditional territories and reserves in the Okanagan region of southern British Columbia.

Wet'suwet'en (725)
Pronounced "wet-soo-wet-on." Formerly known as Broman Lake. Traditional territories in west-central British Columbia.

Whispering Pines/Clinton (702)
Traditional territories and reserves in central British
Columbia, near Clinton.

Williams Lake (719)
Traditional territories and reserves in central British
Columbia, near Williams Lake.

Wuikinuxv. See *Oweekeno/Wuikinuxv Nation.*

Xaxli'p (592)
Pronounced "HAA-clip" or "hawk-leap." Also known
as Fountain. Traditional territories and reserves in the
southern interior, near Lillooet.

Xeni Gwet'in (714)
Pronounced "ha-nay gwet-en" or "hon-ay gwi-teen."
Traditional territories and reserves in central British
Columbia.

Xwemalhkwu. See *Homalco.*

Yakweakwioose (576)
Pronounced "ya-kweek-we-oos." Traditional territories
and reserves in the Fraser Valley region of southwestern
British Columbia.

Yale (589)
Traditional territories and reserves in the Fraser Canyon
region of southwestern British Columbia.

Yekooche (728)
Pronounced "yeh-koo-chee." Also known as Yekootchet'en.
Traditional territories and reserves in central British
Columbia.

Yunesit'in (717)
Pronounced "you-neh-seh-teen." Formerly known as
Stone. Traditional territories and reserves in central
British Columbia.

Yuułuʔiłʔatḥ. See *Ucluelet.*

Appendix 2
Major Ethnic Groups

Ethnic groups among First Nations in British Columbia are defined primarily by language and culture. However, there is no consensus on either the distinction of major ethnic groups or the specific nations within the larger ethnic groups. Some major ethnic groups consist of a single First Nation, while others are made up of multiple First Nations. Pronunciations are based on guides published by the provincial and federal governments.

Babine. See *Nat'oot'en.*

Beaver. See *Dunne-za.*

Bella Bella. See *Heiltsuk.*

Bella Coola. See *Nuxalk.*

Burrard. See *Tsleil-Waututh.*

Carrier. See *Dakelh.*

Champagne and Aishihik
Traditional territories are mostly in the Yukon but extend into northwestern British Columbia.

Chilcotin. See *Tsilhqot'in.*

Comox. See *K'omoks.*

Dakelh
Pronounced "da-kel" or "ka-kel." Formerly known as Carrier. Traditional territories are in central British Columbia. Member nations are ?Esdilagh, Burns Lake, Cheslatta Carrier, Kluskus, Lheidli T'enneh, Lhtako Dene, Nadleh Whut'en, Nak'azdli, Nazko, Saik'uz, Stellat'en, Takla Lake, Tl'azt'en, Ulkatcho, and Yekooche.

Dene-thah
Pronounced "de-ney-ta." Formerly known as Slave or

Slavey. Traditional territories are in northeastern British Columbia. Many of the nations in this part of the province represent a mixture of Dene-thah, Dunne-za, and Sekani ethnic origins. Those nations are Blueberry River, Doig River, Fort Nelson, Halfway River, Kwadacha, McLeod Lake, Prophet River, Tsay Keh Dene, and West Moberly.

Ditidaht. See *Nuu'chah'nulth.*

Dunne-za

Pronounced "de-ney-za." Formerly known as Beaver. Traditional territories are in northeastern British Columbia. Many of the nations in this part of the province represent a mixture of Dene-thah, Dunne-za, and Sekani ethnic origins. Those nations are Blueberry River, Doig River, Fort Nelson, Halfway River, Kwadacha, McLeod Lake, Prophet River, Tsay Key Dene, and West Moberly.

Gitxsan

Pronounced "git-san." Traditional territories are in northwestern British Columbia, around the Skeena River. Member nations are Gitanmaax, Gitanyow, Gitsegukla, Gitwangak, Glen Vowell, and Kispiox.

Haida

Pronounced "hy-dah." Traditional territories encompass Haida Gwaii. Member nations are Old Massett Village Council and Skidegate.

Haisla

Pronounced "hyzlah." Also known as Kitimat or Kitamaat. Traditional territories are on the central mainland coast.

Halq'emeylem (including Sto:lo, Musqueam, and Tsawwassen)

Traditional territories are in southeastern British Columbia. Member nations are Katzie, Kwikwetlem, Musqueam, New Westminster, Semiahmoo, Shxw'ow'hamel, Sts'ailes, Tsawwassen, and Yale. The Halq'emeylem also includes nations commonly associated with Sto:lo: Aitchelitz,

Chawathil, Cheam, Kwantlen, Kwaw-kwaw-Apilt, Leqá:mel, Matsqui, Peters, Popkum, Scowlitz, Seabird Island, Shxwha:y Village, Shxw'ow'hamel, Skawahlook, Skowkale, Skwah, Soowahlie, Squiala, Sumas, Tzeachten, Union Bar, and Yakweakwioose.

Heiltsuk
Pronounced "hail-tsuk." Formerly known as Bella Bella. Traditional territories are on the central coast.

Homalco
Traditional territories are around Bute Inlet on the south-central mainland coast. The Homalco have sometimes been considered part of the Kwakwaka'wakw.

Hul'qumi'num
Pronounced "hul-ka-mee-num." Traditional territories are north of the Straits Salish in and around southeastern Vancouver Island. Member nations are Cowichan, Halalt, Lake Cowichan, Lyackson, Malahat, Nanoose, and Penelakut, Snuneymuxw, and Stz'uminus.

Inland Tlingit. See *Taku Tlingit.*

Kaska
Traditional territories are in northern British Columbia and the Yukon. The member nation in British Columbia is Dease River.

Kitimat, Kitamaat. See *Haisla.*

Klahoose
Traditional territories are around Cortez Island and the adjacent mainland area of the south-central coast. The Klahoose are sometimes considered to be part of Kwakwaka'wakw.

K'omoks
Also known as Comox. Traditional territories are on the central east coast of Vancouver Island. The K'omoks are considered by some to be part of Kwakwaka'wakw.

Kootenay. See *Ktunaxa.*

Ktunaxa

Pronounced "tun-ah-hah." Formerly known as Kootenay or Kutenai. Traditional territories are in southeastern British Columbia. Member nations are ?Akisq'nuk, Lower Kootenay, St Mary's, and Tobacco Plains.

Kutenai. See *Ktunaxa.*

Kwagiulth, Kwakiutl. See *Kwakwaka'wakw.*

Kwakwaka'wakw

Pronounced "kwak-wak-ya-wak" or "kwalk-walk-ya-walk-wuh." Formerly known as Kwakiutl and Kwagiulth. Traditional territories cover northeastern Vancouver Island and adjacent mainland. Member nations are Campbell River, Cape Mudge, Da'naxda'xw, Dzawada'enuxw, Gwa'sala-Nakwaxda'xw, Kwakiutl, Kwiakah, Mamalilikulla-Qwe'Qwa'Sot'Em, Namgis, Qualicum, Quatsino, Tlatlasikwala, and Tlowitsis. The K'omoks (Comox), Homalco, and Klahoose nations have sometimes been considered Kwakwaka'wakw.

Lake Babine. See *Nat'oot'en.*

Lillooet. See *Stl'atl'imx.*

Lil'wet'ul. See *Stl'atl'imx.*

Musqueam

Often considered part of Halq'emeylem. Traditional territories of Musqueam are in and around Vancouver.

Nat'oot'en

Formerly known as Babine and Lake Babine. Traditional territories are in north-central British Columbia.

Nisga'a

Pronounced "nis-gah." Formerly known as Niska and Nishga. Traditional territories are in the area of the Nass River in northwest British Columbia. With the implementation of the Nisga'a Treaty in 2000, formalized Nisga'a "bands" ceased to exist. Major groupings are the Nisga'a villages of Gingolx, Gitwinksihlkw, Laxgalt'sap, and New Aiyansh.

Nlaka'pamux

Pronounced "ing-khla-kap-muh." Formerly known as Thompson. Traditional territories are in the southern interior of British Columbia. Member nations are Ashcroft, Boothroyd, Boston Bar, Cook's Ferry, Kanaka Bar, Lytton, Nicomen, Oregon Jack Creek, Siska, Skuppah, and Spuzzum. Four nations of the Nicola Valley – Coldwater, Lower Nicola, Nooaitch, and Shackan – are sometimes considered part of Nlaka'pamux.

Nootka. See *Nuu'chah'nulth.*

Nuu'chah'nulth

Pronounced "new-cha-nulth." Formerly known as Nootka. Traditional territories are on the west coast of Vancouver Island and adjacent islands and inland areas. Member nations are Ahousaht, Ehattesaht, Hesquiaht, Hupacasath, Huu-ay-aht, Ka:'yu:'k't'h'/Che:k:tles7et'h', Mowachat/Muchalaht, Nuchatlaht, Tla-o-qui-aht, Toquaht, Tseshaht, Uchucklesaht, and Ucluelet. The Pacheedaht and Ditidaht are sometimes considered member nations.

Nuxalk

Pronounced "nu-halk" or "noo-hulk." Formerly known as Bella Coola. Traditional territories are on the central mainland coast.

Okanagan

Traditional territories are in the Okanagan region of south-central British Columbia. Member nations are Lower Similkameen, Okanagan, Osoyoos, Penticton, Upper Similkameen, and Westbank. The Upper Nicola are sometimes considered Okanagan.

Oweekeno

Pronounced "o-wik-en-o." Also known as Wuikinuxv. Traditional territories are in the central coast region.

Pacheedaht. See *Nuu'chah'nulth.*

Sechelt

Pronounced "sea-shelt." Also known as Shishalh. Traditional territories are around Sechelt on the southern mainland coast.

Secwepemc

Pronounced "she-whep-m" or "shi-huep-much" or "she-kwe-pem." Formerly known as Shuswap. Traditional territories are in the southern interior of British Columbia. Member nations are Adams Lake, Bonaparte, Canim Lake, Esk'etemc, High Bar, Little Shuswap Lake, Neskonlith, Simpcw, Skeetchestn, Soda Creek, Splatsin, Stswecem'c Xgat'tem, Tk'emlups te Secwepemc, Ts'kw'aylaxw, Whispering Pines/Clinton, and Williams Lake.

Sekani

Pronounced "sik-an-ee" or "seh-kah-nee." Traditional territories are in northeastern British Columbia. Many of the nations in this part of the province represent a mixture of Dene-thah, Dunne-za, and Sekani ethnic origins. Those nations are Blueberry River, Doig River, Fort Nelson, Halfway River, Kwadacha, McLeod Lake, Prophet River, Tsay Keh Dene, and West Moberly.

Shishalh. See *Sechelt.*

Shuswap. See *Secwepemc.*

Slave, or *Slavey.* See *Dene-thah.*

Sliammon

Pronounced "sligh-am-un." Traditional territories are around Powell River on the south-central mainland coast.

Squamish

Pronounced "skwa-mish." Traditional territories are in southeastern British Columbia, extending from Vancouver to Whistler and encompassing areas around Howe Sound.

Stl'atl'imx

Pronounced "stat-liem" or "stat-lee-um." Formerly known as Lillooet. Traditional territories are in the southern interior of British Columbia. Member nations are Bridge River, Cayoose Creek, Douglas, N'Quatqua, Samahquam, Seton Lake, Skatin, T'it'q'et, Ts'kw'aylaxw, and Xaxli'p. Mount Currie is sometimes considered Stl'atl'imx and sometimes as a distinct group known as Lil'wet'ul.

Sto:lo
Pronounced "stoh-lo." The traditional territories of the Sto:lo are in southeastern British Columbia, around the Fraser River Valley. See also *Halq'emeylem.*

Straits Salish
Traditional territories are on southeastern Vancouver Island and adjacent islands. Member nations are Beecher Bay, Esquimalt, Pauquachin, Songhees, Tsartlip, Tsawout, Tseycum, and T'Souke.

Tahltan
Pronounced "tall-tan." Traditional territories are in northwest British Columbia. Member nations are Iskut and Tahltan.

Taku Tlingit
Pronounced "ta-koo kling-git." Formerly known as Inland Tlingit. Traditional territories in northwestern British Columbia.

Thompson. See *Nlaka'pamux.*

Tsawwassen. See *Halq'emeylem.*

Tsilhqot'in
Pronounced "tsill-coat-ten." Formerly known as Chilcotin. Traditional territories are in the Chilcotin area in south-central British Columbia. Member nations are Alexis Creek, Tl'etinqox-t'in, Toosey, Xeni Gwet'in, and Yunesit'in.

Tsimshian
Pronounced "sim-she-an." Traditional territories are in the northern coastal region. Member nations are Gitga'at,

Gitxaala, Kitasoo, Kitselas, Kitsumkalum, Lax-Kw'alaams, and Metlakatla.

Tsleil-Waututh
Pronounced "tslay-wah-tooth." Formerly known as Burrard. Traditional territories are around Burrard Inlet and Indian Arm in the south coast region.

Wet'suwet'en
Pronounced "wet-soo-wet-on." Sometimes considered part of Dakelh. Traditional territories are in west-central British Columbia. Member nations are Hagwilget, Moricetown, Nee-Tahi-Buhn, and Wet'suwet'en.

Wuikinuxv. See *Oweekeno.*

Appendix 3
Excerpts from the British Columbia Heritage Conservation Act, 1996

1   In this Act:

... "first nation" means, as the context requires, an aboriginal people sharing a common traditional territory and having a common traditional language, culture and laws, or the duly mandated governing body of one or more such people; ...

"heritage object" means, whether designated or not, personal property that has heritage value to British Columbia, a community or an aboriginal people;

"heritage site" means, whether designated or not, land, including land covered by water, that has heritage value to British Columbia, a community, or an aboriginal people;

"heritage value" means the historical, cultural, aesthetic, scientific or educational worth or usefulness of a site or object; ...

2   The purpose of this Act is to encourage and facilitate the protection and conservation of heritage property in British Columbia.

[...]

4   (1) The Province may enter into a formal agreement with a first nation with respect to the conservation and protection of heritage sites and heritage objects that represent the cultural heritage of the aboriginal people who are represented by that first nation.

[...]

(4) Without limiting subsection (1), an agreement made under this section may include one or more of the following:

(a) a schedule of heritage sites and heritage objects that
are of particular spiritual, ceremonial or other cultural value to the aboriginal people for the purpose
of protection under section 13 (2) (h);

(b) a schedule of heritage sites and objects of cultural
value to the aboriginal people that are not included
in a schedule under paragraph (a); ...

[...]

6   If, with respect to any matter affecting the conservation of a
heritage site or heritage object referred to in section 13 (2),
there is a conflict between this Act and any other Act, this
Act prevails.

[...]

8.1 If a treaty first nation, in accordance with its final agreement,
makes laws for the conservation and protection of, and access to, heritage sites and heritage objects on its treaty lands,
sections 9, 12, 13, 14, 16, 18 and 20 (1) (a) do not apply
in relation to those treaty lands.

9   (1) The Lieutenant Governor in Council may
(a) designate land as a Provincial heritage site, or
(b) designate an object as a Provincial heritage object.

[...]

11   (1) If a designation under section 9 causes, or will cause at
the time of designation, a reduction in the market value
of the designated property, the government must com-
pensate an owner of the designated property who makes
an application under subsection (2), and the compensation must be in an amount or in a form the minister
and the owner agree on or, failing an agreement, in an
amount or in a form determined by binding arbitration
under subsection (4).

(2) The owner of a designated property may apply to the
minister for compensation for the reduction in the
market value of the designated property.

(3) An application under subsection (2)

(a) must be made, in order for the owner to be entitled to compensation under this section, no later than one year after the designation under section 9, and

(b) may be made before the designation under section 9.

[...]

(9) This section does not apply to property that, immediately before its designation under section 9, is

(a) designated as a Provincial heritage site,

(b) designated as a heritage object,

(c) protected under section 13 (2), or

(d) designated under section 967 of the *Local Government Act* or section 593 of the *Vancouver Charter*.

[...]

13 (1) Except as authorized by a permit issued under section 12 or 14, a person must not remove, or attempt to remove, from British Columbia a heritage object that is protected under subsection (2) or which has been removed from a site protected under subsection (2).

(2) Except as authorized by a permit issued under section 12 or 14, or an order issued under section 14, a person must not do any of the following:

(a) damage, desecrate or alter a Provincial heritage site or a Provincial heritage object or remove from a Provincial heritage site or Provincial heritage object any heritage object or material that constitutes part of the site or object;

(b) damage, desecrate or alter a burial place that has historical or archaeological value or remove human remains or any heritage object from a burial place that has historical or archaeological value;

(c) damage, alter, cover or move an aboriginal rock painting or aboriginal rock carving that has historical or archaeological value;

(d) damage, excavate, dig in or alter, or remove any heritage object from, a site that contains artifacts, features, materials or other physical evidence of human habitation or use before 1846;

(e) damage or alter a heritage wreck or remove any heritage object from a heritage wreck; ...

[...]

36 (1) A person who does any of the following commits an offence:

[...]

(d) contravenes section 13 (1) or (2).

[...]

(3) A person convicted of an offence under subsection (1) (d) is liable,

(a) if the person is an individual, to a fine of not more than $50,000 or to imprisonment for a term of not more than 2 years or to both, or

(b) if the person is a corporation, to a fine of not more than $1,000,000.

(4) If a corporation commits an offence under this Act, an employee, officer, director or agent of the corporation who authorized, permitted or acquiesced in the offence also commits the offence and is liable.

Appendix 4
Apology for Residential Schools

This is an excerpt from the apology by the Canadian government for the Indian residential school system. It was read by Prime Minister Stephen Harper in Parliament on June 11, 2008.

APOLOGY ON BEHALF OF CANADIANS FOR THE
INDIAN RESIDENTIAL SCHOOL SYSTEM

The treatment of children in Indian Residential Schools is a sad chapter in our history.

For more than a century, Indian Residential Schools separated over 150,000 Aboriginal children from their families and communities. In the 1870s, the federal government, partly in order to meet its obligation to educate Aboriginal children, began to play a role in the development and administration of these schools. Two primary objectives of the Residential Schools system were to remove and isolate children from the influence of their homes, families, traditions, and cultures, and to assimilate them into the dominant culture. These objectives were based on the assumption Aboriginal cultures and spiritual beliefs were inferior and unequal. Indeed, some sought, as it was infamously said, "to kill the Indian in the child." Today, we recognize that this policy of assimilation was wrong, has caused great harm, and has no place in our country.

One hundred and thirty-two federally supported schools were located in every province and territory, except Newfoundland, New Brunswick and Prince Edward Island. Most schools were operated as "joint ventures" with Anglican, Catholic,

Presbyterian or United Churches. The Government of Canada built an educational system in which very young children were often forcibly removed from their homes, often taken far from their communities. Many were inadequately fed, clothed and housed. All were deprived of the care and nurturing of their parents, grandparents and communities. First Nations, Inuit and Métis languages and cultural practices were prohibited in these schools. Tragically, some of these children died while attending residential schools and others never returned home.

The government now recognizes that the consequences of the Indian Residential Schools policy were profoundly negative and that this policy has had a lasting and damaging impact on Aboriginal culture, heritage and language. While some former students have spoken positively about their experiences at residential schools, these stories are far overshadowed by tragic accounts of the emotional, physical and sexual abuse and neglect of helpless children, and their separation from powerless families and communities.

The legacy of Indian Residential Schools has contributed to social problems that continue to exist in many communities today.

It has taken extraordinary courage for the thousands of survivors that have come forward to speak publicly about the abuse they suffered. It is a testament to their resilience as individuals and to the strength of their cultures. Regrettably, many former students are not with us today and died never having received a full apology from the Government of Canada.

The government recognizes that the absence of an apology has been an impediment to healing and reconciliation. Therefore, on behalf of the Government of Canada and all Canadians, I stand before you, in this Chamber so central to our life as a country, to apologize to Aboriginal peoples for Canada's role in the Indian Residential Schools system.

To the approximately 80,000 living former students, and all family members and communities, the Government of Canada now recognizes that it was wrong to forcibly remove children from their homes and we apologize for having done this. We now recognize that it was wrong to separate children from rich and vibrant cultures and traditions, that it created a void in many lives and communities, and we apologize for having done this. We now recognize that, in separating children from their families, we undermined the ability of many to adequately parent their own children and sowed the seeds for generations to follow, and we apologize for having done this. We now recognize that, far too often, these institutions gave rise to abuse or neglect and were inadequately controlled, and we apologize for failing to protect you. Not only did you suffer these abuses as children, but as you became parents, you were powerless to protect your own children from suffering the same experience, and for this we are sorry.

The burden of this experience has been on your shoulders for far too long. The burden is properly ours as a Government, and as a country. There is no place in Canada for the attitudes that inspired the Indian Residential Schools system to ever prevail again. You have been working on recovering from this experience for a long time, and in a very real sense we are now joining you on this journey. The Government of Canada sincerely apologizes and asks forgiveness of the Aboriginal peoples of this country for failing them so profoundly.

Nous le regrettons
We are sorry
Nimitataynan
Niminchinowesamin
Mamiattugut

Appendix 5
Excerpts from the Royal Proclamation, 1763

By the King, a Royal Proclamation

Whereas We have taken into Our Royal Consideration the extensive and valuable Acquisitions in America, secured to our Crown by the late Definitive Treaty of Peace, concluded at Paris, the 10th Day of February last; and being desirous that all Our loving Subjects, as well of our Kingdom as of our Colonies in America, may avail themselves with all convenient Speed, of the great Benefits and Advantages which must accrue therefrom to their Commerce, Manufactures, and Navigation, We have thought fit, with the Advice of our Privy Council, to issue this our Royal Proclamation ...

And whereas it is just and reasonable, and essential to our Interest, and the Security of our Colonies, that the several Nations or Tribes of Indians with whom We are connected, and who live under our Protection, should not be molested or disturbed in the Possession of such Parts of Our Dominion and Territories as, not having been ceded to or purchased by Us, are reserved to them, or any of them, as their Hunting Grounds ...

And We do further declare it to be Our Royal Will and Pleasure, for the present as aforesaid, to reserve under our Sovereignty, Protection, and Dominion, for the use of the said Indians, all the Lands and Territories not included within the Limits of Our said Three new Governments, or within the Limits of the Territory granted to the Hudson's Bay Company, as also all the Lands and Territories lying to the Westward of the Sources of the Rivers which fall into the Sea from the West and North West as aforesaid.

And We do hereby strictly forbid, on Pain of our Displeasure, all our loving Subjects from making any Purchases or Settlements whatever, or taking Possession of any Lands above reserved, without our especial leave and Licence for that Purpose first obtained. And we do further strictly enjoin and require all Persons whatever who have either wilfully or inadvertently seated themselves upon any Lands within the Countries above described, or upon any other Lands which, not having been ceded to or purchased by Us, are still reserved to the said Indians as aforesaid, forthwith to remove themselves from such settlements.

And whereas great Frauds and Abuses have been committed in purchasing Lands of the Indians, to the great Prejudice of our Interests, and to the great Dissatisfaction of the said Indians; In order, therefore to prevent such Irregularities for the future, and to the end that the Indians may be convinced of our Justice, and determined Resolution to remove all reasonable Cause of Discontent, We do, with the Advice of our Privy Council, strictly enjoin and require, that no private Person do presume to make any purchases from the said Indians of any lands reserved to the said Indians, within those parts of our Colonies where, We have thought Proper to allow Settlement; but that, if at any Time any of the Said Indians should be inclined to dispose of the said Lands, the same shall be purchased only for Us, in our Name, at some public Meeting or Assembly of the said Indians, to be held for the Purpose by the Governor or Commander in Chief of our Colony respectively within which they shall lie ...

Given at our Court of St. James the 7th Day of October 1763, in the Third Year of our Reign.

God Save the King

Glossary

Aboriginal. As defined by the Canadian Constitution, all Indigenous people of Canada, including Indians (status and non-status), Métis, and Inuit people.

Aboriginal rights. The rights of Aboriginal peoples, subject to negotiation or adjudication. The Canadian Constitution protects "aboriginal rights" but fails to state the nature of those rights. Rights may include the freedom to maintain traditional economic and social activities as well as rights to lands, resources, and self-government.

Anthropology. The study of humans from evolutionary, comparative, and holistic perspectives.

Archaeological site. Any location where there is physical evidence of past human activity. Locations in British Columbia are rarely designated as archaeological sites unless they are at least 100 years old, and are not protected by legislation unless they predate 1846.

Archaeology. The branch of anthropology that focuses on the activities of humans in the past, through the analysis of the physical evidence of their activities.

Artifact. An object, usually portable, that shows evidence of being made or used by people.

Band. As defined in the Indian Act (1985): "A body of Indians … for whose use and benefit in common, lands, the legal title to which is vested in Her Majesty, have been set apart." Many bands are now referred to as nations.

Beringia. A large area of land covering portions of northwestern North America and northeastern Asia that remained ice-free during the last ice age. Most archaeologists believe that Beringia was the first area within the Americas to have been inhabited by people.

Biological anthropology. The branch of anthropology that focuses on human biology, past and present.

Blood quantum. The percentage or proportion of First Nations blood a person has.

Coast Salish. The grouping used to describe several major ethnic groups and dozens of First Nations occupying the south coastal mainland, southeast Vancouver Island, and the islands in between. The major ethnic groups usually considered as being Coast Salish include the Halq'emeylem (Musqueam, Sto:lo, and Tsawwassen), Homalco, Hul'qumi'num, Klahoose, Sechelt, Squamish, Straits Salish, and Tsleil-Waututh.

Colonialism. The process of a European nation occupying a land already occupied by Indigenous people and then subjugating and dominating them.

Cultural anthropology. The branch of anthropology focusing on cultures of the present and recent past.

Cultural appropriation. A group taking elements of another group's culture and then using it for its own purposes. An example is governments and corporations using totem poles in tourism marketing.

Cultural resource management (CRM). The identification, assessment, excavation, or protection of archaeological sites that are under threat of destruction by natural or cultural agency. Also called commercial archaeology.

Culture. Everything that people learn and share as members of a society. Culture includes, but is not limited to, languages, values, beliefs, social organization, customs, economic strategies, and technology. Cultures are dynamic and fluid rather than static. They are continually changing while maintaining core elements.

Culture area. A geographic region in which separate societies have similar cultures. The culture areas in British Columbia were the Northwest Coast, the Interior Plateau, and the Subarctic.

Ethnography. Written description of a society based on either the first-hand observation of the writer (the ethnographer) or the memories of individuals.

First Nation. A self-determined group comprising the descendants of people who lived in what is now British Columbia before the arrival of Europeans and Americans in the late eighteenth century. In many instances the term "First Nation" has replaced "Indian band."

Indian. One of three kinds of Aboriginal people recognized in the Canadian Constitution (along with Inuit and Métis). Historically, a term widely used to describe the descendants of the first inhabitants of the Americas. Also known as First Nations, Natives, Aboriginal people, and Indigenous people.

Indian Act. The federal act governing relations between First Nations and government.

Indigenous. Globally, the term is used to refer to minority populations that can trace their ancestry into the distant past, and are now dominated by others. In North America, the term includes the Aboriginal peoples of Canada (First Nations/ Indian, Inuit, and Métis) and Native Americans (Indians, Aleuts, Eskimos).

Interior Salish. Grouping used to describe some of the major ethnic groups and dozens of First Nations in the southern interior of British Columbia, including the First Nations affiliated with the Nlaka'pamux, Okanagan, Secwepemc, and Stl'atl'imx.

Linguistic anthropology. The branch of anthropology that focuses on languages.

Midden. A common feature of archaeological sites, comprising the accumulated trash of a settlement. When the midden contains a visible proportion of shell, it is often referred to as a shell midden. Thousands of middens are recorded in British Columbia.

Myth. A story that involves the activities of characters whom non-First Nations people would usually describe as supernatural. In anthropology, referring to a story as a myth is not a judgment about whether the story is true; rather, it indicates that it involves characters who are able to do things ordinary people or animals cannot.

Non-status Indian. A person of First Nations descent who is not recognized as Indian by the federal government. Non-status

Indians are not governed by the Indian Act. While they may affiliate with a particular ethnic group, they are rarely members of a specific, registered First Nation.

Prehistory. Before written records. For most of British Columbia the transition from prehistory to history occurs in the late eighteenth and early nineteenth centuries, when Europeans and Americans coming from societies that had writing first encountered First Nations.

Recall ethnography. Documenting lifeways based on the recollections of people. This is how much of the ethnographic work in British Columbia in the late 1800s and early 1900s was undertaken – anthropologists writing down the recollections and stories community members told about lifeways in the past.

Registered Indian. A person whose name appears on a register maintained by the federal government. Registered Indians are governed by the Indian Act.

Reserve. An allotment of land set aside by the federal government for Indians. There are approximately 1,500 reserves in British Columbia. The federal government has jurisdiction over reserves.

Residential schools. Boarding schools for First Nations children, run by religious organizations, were the policy of the federal government, primarily to hasten the process of assimilation. The schools, which have largely been judged a failure, resulted in extensive abuse of First Nations children and left a long and devastating legacy. The last residential school in British Columbia closed in the 1980s.

Salvage ethnography. Ethnographic research on traditional cultures that is done before they are forever changed. Most ethnographic research done in the late 1800s and early 1900s in British Columbia was salvage ethnography, because anthropologists and others were guided by an understanding that the traditional lifeways and memories of them were rapidly disappearing.

Status Indian. *See* Registered Indian.

Selected Bibliography

In addition to the sources listed here, readers are encouraged to peruse *B.C. Studies*, which regularly publishes scholarly articles on First Nations people, cultures, and issues in British Columbia. Information on First Nations is also accessible through government websites. The website address of the provincial Ministry of Aboriginal Relations and Reconciliation is www.gov.bc.ca/arr. The website address of Aboriginal Affairs and Northern Development Canada is www.aadnc-aandc.gc.ca.

Ames, Kenneth M., and Herbert D.G. Maschner. *Peoples of the Northwest Coast: Their Archaeology and Prehistory.* New York: Thames and Hudson, 1999.

Barman, Jean. *Stanley Park's Secret: The Forgotten Families of Whoi Whoi, Kanaka Ranch and Brockton Point.* Madeira Park, BC: Harbour Publishing, 2005.

–. *The West beyond the West: A History of British Columbia.* Rev. ed. Toronto: University of Toronto Press, 1996.

Berkhofer, Robert, Jr. *The White Man's Indian: Images of the American Indian from Columbus to the Present.* New York: Vintage, 1978.

Biolsi, Thomas, ed. *A Companion to the Anthropology of American Indians.* Malden, MA: Blackwell, 2008.

Brody, Hugh. *Maps and Dreams: Indians and the British Columbia Frontier.* Vancouver: Douglas and McIntyre, 1988.

Campbell, Kenneth, Charles Menzies, and Brent Peacock. *B.C. First Nations Studies.* Victoria: BC Ministry of Education, 2003.

Carleton, Sean. "Colonizing Minds: Public Education, the 'Textbook Indian,' and Settler Colonialism in British Columbia, 1920-1970." *BC Studies* 169 (2011): 101-30.

Carlson, Keith Thor. *The Power of Place, the Problem of Time: Aboriginal Identity and Historical Consciousness in the Cauldron of Colonialism.* Toronto: University of Toronto Press, 2010.

Carlson, Roy L., and Luke Dalla Bona, eds. *Early Human Occupation in British Columbia*. Vancouver: UBC Press, 1996.

Clark, Donald W. *Western Subarctic Prehistory*. Hull, QC: Canadian Museum of Civilization, 1991.

Cote, Charlotte. *Spirits of Our Whaling Ancestors: Revitalizing Makah and Nuu-chah-nulth Traditions*. Seattle: University of Washington Press, 2010.

Culhane, Dara. *The Pleasure of the Crown: Anthropology, Law and First Nations*. Vancouver: Talonbooks, 1998.

Deloria, Philip. *Playing Indian*. New Haven, CT: Yale University Press, 1988.

Deloria, Vine, Jr. *Custer Died for Your Sins: An Indian Manifesto*. Norman: University of Oklahoma Press, 1969.

Deur, Douglas, and Nancy Turner, eds. *Keeping It Living: Traditions of Plant Use and Cultivation on the Northwest Coast of North America*. Vancouver: UBC Press, 2005.

Duff, Wilson. *The Indian History of British Columbia*. Vol. 1, *The Impact of the White Man*. Anthropology in British Columbia Memoir no. 5. Victoria: BC Provincial Museum, 1965.

Fisher, Robin. *Contact and Conflict: Indian-European Relations in British Columbia, 1774-1890*. 2nd ed. Vancouver: UBC Press, 1992.

Fladmark, Knut. *British Columbia Prehistory*. Ottawa: National Museums of Canada, 1986.

Forte, Maximilian, ed. *Who Is an Indian? Race, Place, and the Politics of Indigeneity in the Americas*. Toronto: University of Toronto Press, 2013.

Francis, Daniel. *The Imaginary Indian: The Image of the Indian in Canadian Culture*. 2nd ed. Vancouver: Arsenal Pulp Press, 2011.

Furniss, Elizabeth. *The Burden of History: Colonialism and the Frontier Myth in a Rural Canadian Community*. Vancouver: UBC Press, 1999.

Garroutte, Eva Marie. *Real Indians: Identity and the Survival of Native America*. Berkeley: University of California Press, 2003.

Gray, Lynda. *First Nations 101: Tons of Stuff You Need to Know about First Nations People*. Vancouver: Adaawx Publishing, 2011.

Haig-Brown, Celia. *Resistance and Renewal: Surviving the Indian Residential School*. Vancouver: Tillicum, 1988.

Halpin, Marjorie. *Totem Poles: An Illustrated Guide*. Vancouver: UBC Press and the UBC Museum of Anthropology, 1981.

Harris, Cole. *Making Native Space: Colonialism, Resistance, and Reserves in British Columbia*. Vancouver: UBC Press, 2002.

Hedican, Edward J. *Applied Anthropology in Canada: Understanding Aboriginal Issues*. 2nd ed. Toronto: University of Toronto Press, 2008.

–. *Ipperwash: The Tragic Failure of Canada's Aboriginal Policy*. Toronto: University of Toronto Press, 2013.

Helm, June, ed. *Subarctic*. Vol. 6 of *Handbook of North American Indians*. Washington, DC: Smithsonian Institution, 1981.

Hill, Gord. *500 Years of Indigenous Resistance*. Oakland, CA: PM Press, 2009.

–. *The 500 Years of Resistance Comic Book*. Vancouver: Arsenal Pulp Press, 2010.

Jensen, Vickie. *The Totem Poles of Stanley Park*. Vancouver: Westcoast Words, 2009.

Johnston, Hugh J.M., ed. *The Pacific Province: A History of British Columbia*. Vancouver: Douglas and McIntyre, 1996.

Jonaitis, Aldona. *Art of the Northwest Coast*. Vancouver: Douglas and McIntyre, 2006.

Jonaitis, Aldona, and Aaron Glass. *The Totem Pole: An Intercultural History*. Vancouver: Douglas and McIntyre, 2010.

Kleer, Nancy, Kate Kempton, Renee Pelletier, Bryce Edwards, Maggie Wente, Larry Innes, Cathy Guirguis, et al. *Aboriginal Law Handbook*. 4th ed. Toronto: Carswell, 2012.

Knight, Rolf. *Indians at Work: An Informal History of Native Labour in British Columbia, 1848-1930*. Vancouver: New Star Books, 1996.

Lillard, Charles, and Terry Glavin. *A Voice Great within Us*. Vancouver: New Star Books, 1998.

Lutz, John Sutton. *Makúk: A New History of Aboriginal-White Relations*. Vancouver: UBC Press, 2008.

Matson, R.G., and Gary Coupland. *Prehistory of the Northwest Coast*. New York: Academic Press, 1994.

Matson, R.G., Gary Coupland, and Quentin Mackie, eds. *Emerging from the Mist: Studies in Northwest Coast Culture History*. Vancouver: UBC Press, 2003.

Maud, Ralph. *A Guide to B.C. Indian Myth and Legend.* Vancouver: Talonbooks, 1982.

Mauze, Marie, Michael E. Harkin, and Sergei Kan, eds. *Coming to Shore: Northwest Coast Ethnology, Traditions, and Visions.* Lincoln: University of Nebraska Press, 2004.

McIlwraith, Thomas. *"We Are Still Didene": Stories of Hunting and History from Northern British Columbia.* Toronto: University of Toronto Press, 2012.

Menzies, Charles R., ed. *Traditional Ecological Knowledge and Natural Resource Management.* Lincoln: University of Nebraska Press, 2006.

Miller, J.R. *Shingwauk's Vision: A History of Native Residential Schools.* Toronto: University of Toronto Press, 1996.

Moss, Madonna L. *Northwest Coast: Archaeology as Deep History.* Washington, DC: Society for American Archaeology, 2011.

Muckle, Robert. *The Indigenous Peoples of North America: A Concise Anthropological Overview.* Toronto: University of Toronto Press, 2012.

Prentiss, Anna Marie, and Ian Kuijt. *People of the Middle Fraser Canyon: An Archaeological History.* Vancouver: UBC Press, 2012.

Ray, Arthur J. *I Have Lived Here since the World Began: An Illustrated History of Canada's Native People.* Toronto: Lester Publishing and Key Porter Books, 1996.

Ridington, Robin. "Re-Creation in Canadian First Nation Literatures: 'When You Sing It Now, Just Like New.'" *Anthropologica* 43, 2 (2001): 221-30.

Roy, Susan. *These Mysterious People: Shaping History and Archaeology in a Northwest Coast Community.* Montreal: McGill-Queen's University Press, 2010.

Stewart, Hilary. *Looking at Indian Art of the Northwest Coast.* Vancouver: Douglas and McIntyre, 1979.

–. *Totem Poles.* Vancouver: Douglas and McIntyre, 1990.

Suttles, Wayne, ed. *Northwest Coast.* Vol. 7 of *Handbook of North American Indians.* Washington, DC: Smithsonian Institution, 1990.

Swanky, Tom. *The True Story of Canada's "War" of Extermination on the Pacific, plus the Tsilhqot'in and Other First Nations Resistance.* Burnaby, BC: Dragon Heart Enterprises, 2012.

Tennant, Paul. *Aboriginal Peoples and Politics: The Indian Land Question in British Columbia, 1849-1989.* Vancouver: UBC Press, 1990.

Tindall, D.B., Ronald L. Trosper, and Pamela Perrault, eds. *Aboriginal Peoples and Forest Lands in Canada.* Vancouver: UBC Press, 2013.

Turner, Nancy. *Food Plants of Coastal First Peoples.* Vancouver: UBC Press, 1995.

–. *Food Plants of Interior First Peoples.* Vancouver: UBC Press, 1997.

–. *Plant Technology of First Peoples in British Columbia.* Vancouver: UBC Press, 1998.

Walker, Deward, ed. *Plateau.* Vol. 12 of *Handbook of North American Indians.* Washington, DC: Smithsonian Institution, 1998.

Warry, Wayne. *Ending Denial: Understanding Aboriginal Issues.* Toronto: University of Toronto Press, 2008.

Webster, Gloria Cranmer. "From Colonization to Repatriation." In *Indigena: Contemporary Native Perspectives,* edited by Gerald McMaster and Lee-Ann Martin, 25-37. Vancouver: Douglas and McIntyre, 1992.

Printed and bound in Canada by Friesens

Set in Giovanni and Univers by Artegraphica Design Co. Ltd.

Copy editor: Sarah Wight

Proofreader: Judy Phillips

Cartographer: Eric Leinberger